We Hillfolk

by

Scott Woods

For my husband

1.

We forged ahead like two confident lemmings leaping off a cliff.

Vincent, an unemployed actor, and I, an unemployed artist, were about to buy a farmstead deep in the Catskill Mountains of Upstate New York.

Seemed like a plan.

Isn't it the dream of every man to carve out a tiny slice of paradise that he can call his own? It had been my dream since early childhood. Our father had instilled in my brothers and me a love of country living. We spent our formative years on the family tree farm at a bend in the road known as Callicoon Center. In those hills we three brothers became educated in such important life skills as damming brooks, shooting pumpkins, and setting fire to outhouses. We bonded with each other and with the countryside.

Now, after ten years of searching for myself in California, I had returned with my life partner to those boyhood hills to carve out a tiny slice of my own.

The dream: a sheltered homestead with clear skies and unspoiled vistas, a secret garden that bosomed with dinner plate dahlias and Yukon gold potatoes, a flat green yard with a picket fence and an outdoor shower and chickens.

Definitely chickens.

You may wonder how on Earth we planned to finance this dream and, looking back, I'm kind of wondering that myself. But we did. We searched the internet and drove the endless back roads on a quest to find our Shangri-La. Now I am not a praying man, but at one point I took a quiet moment to speak to my recently departed father.

"Please Dad... help me find my perfect country home."

The very next day the real estate print-out directed us way into the hills and down a bumpy dirt road to a sadly forgotten clapboard house on fifteen south facing acres at the edge of forever preserved forest. Bleached by time, weathered yet proud, the little house was shuttered tight against the days, waiting, just waiting for the right suckers to come along.

And here we came.

The property around the house was open and flat with three out buildings begging to be unlocked. Beyond them the land sloped down to a pond. Certainly everything was overgrown and needing paint, but as they say the bones were good.

Vincent's chestnut hair tussled in the breeze, his dark eyes gazing.

"Nice view," he said.

It sounds hokey but I swear it's true; at that moment, clouds parted and beams of sunlight shined down on the quirky little farmstead. Surely a sign from dear ol' Dad.

We made an offer without even looking inside the house.

I was on cloud nine. We bought a puppy and a slightly used pick-up truck. It doesn't get any better than that. We named the puppy Poke because she was a pointer and poked her nose into everything and we named the pick-up Rusty because it was.

Before we could trade in our frappuccinos for pitch forks and forever close the chapter on Hollywood, Vincent had to make a quick trip to Los Angeles to finish one final scene on a soap opera. Poke and I would finalize the big real estate deal the next morning at nine o'clock at The First National Bank of Jeffersonville, also known as Jeff Bank. Yes, I was to sign away my life to a bank named Jeff.

The farmstead had been abandoned and no one at the bank seemed to care about it. They already mailed us the key. Tomorrow's board room signing was a mere formality. The house had no furniture but there were beautiful hardwood floors throughout so I borrowed an inflatable mattress from my one brother and a sleeping bag from the other. I'd spend the night alone in the empty house and meet all the suit and tie people at Jeff Bank in the morning.

Poke stood with her paws on the dashboard, happily wagging her tail as I turned onto Laurel Lane. It was all so exciting, about to become a proud home owner. I felt so grown up.

Then up ahead, standing at the edge of the road was my new neighbor.

Now, Vincent and I had already been by the house a couple of times; you know, curtain measuring and pondering paint colors, but we had yet to actually meet any neighbor. This guy's house (well technically, trailer) had always looked tidy. No one was ever around but you could tell someone took pride in the place; the hub caps were hung just so.

He was draping something over the split rail fence as I drove up. *Is that an animal skin?* I slowed to a stop and rolled down the passenger side window.

The guy peered in. He looked mid thirties, with one of those flap-eared caps and a goatee. He wiped the blade of his hunting knife on his camo pants and stashed it into a sheath on his belt. I'm not the biggest guy on the team so I quickly sat up tall, like a real man, and cleared my throat.

"Hello. I'm your new neighbor, Scott."

I had not, until that exact moment, ever realized how gay my name sounds.

The guy reached into the truck to offer a hardy handshake only it didn't turn out too hardy. I kind of misjudged and his big hand grabbed the ends of my dainty artist fingers. Unfortunately, there's no going back. Once you mess up on a handshake you still have to go through with it.

"Hoot. Hoot LeShea."

I wasn't sure I heard him right.

"Hoot?" I asked.

"Hoot," he confirmed.

"Hoot," I repeated.

"Hoot," he repeated.

We sounded like a couple of courting owls.

"You buying the old Plunket place?" Hoot asked.

I wasn't sure; there had been a lot of crossed out names on that deed. I guess I was.

"I use to play with the Plunket kids," Hoot said, his grey eyes lost in the past. "Use to shoot frogs down in that there pond. Me, Whitey and Steven."

Fascinating; what could I say.

Poke, meanwhile, was happy to meet our new neighbor. Her tail was wagging like a Geiger counter needle detecting kryptonite. Hoot rubbed the back of her head.

"This some kind of huntin' dog?"

"Well... yes...," I said. "She's a pointer."

Hoot squared his jaw and asked the question, up in these hills, The Big Question.

"You hunt?"

As I told you earlier, when I was a kid on the tree farm we shot all kinds of guns, but that was then and this was now and I had just spent the past ten years in La La Land. It had been forever since I had shot anything more than a paperclip off a rubber band and Hoot knew it.

"I...ah...well...I'm thinking about training her." I deflected the focus back onto Poke.

Hoot smirked through tight lips. He knew something that I didn't know and it was building up inside of him until he could hold it in no longer.

"You know you're buying a rattlesnake den."

Back on the tree farm we hiked in the hills and rolled in the fields and there were never, ever any rattlesnakes. Obviously this joker was just trying to get a rise out of me. He jerked his head to one side.

"Right down over that bank, between the pond and the house, them big rocks, they den up in there."

He studied me for a reaction. I sat stoic.

"Me and Whitey counted fifty seven one summer."

My mind was racing. Technically, yes, I suppose there could be rattlesnakes in certain parts of New York State, but I never had any encounters. Surely this Hoot character was just trying to get me worked up and I wasn't about to let him. Anyway, the nice people at Jeff Bank never mentioned anything about rattlesnakes. Certainly they would have told me. After all, they told me about the beautiful hardwood floors throughout.

8

I maintained a frozen smile on my face and made like I was shrugging it off but I could sense Hoot watching me squirm. Then he stood up straight and studied the sky.

"Yep," he concluded, "I'd say they should be waking up in a week or two."

Okay, whatever. I had things to do to get ready for tomorrow. I didn't need to listen to this nonsense. I was about to say my goodbyes when Hoot leaned in.

"Say... now I don't want to get in your business but..."

Of course as soon as somebody says that they are in your business.

"...you aware of them rotten beams under that house?"

And that is how I ended up in a crawl space basement with a mountain man named Hoot LeShea stabbing his gargantuan hunting knife into the rotting floor joists of a rattlesnake infested farmhouse that I was about to buy.

"Here."

Stab.

"Here."

Stab.

"Here."

Stab.

"Here."

Bits of wood and dry rot twinkled down like volcanic ash. Hoot seemed to take great pride in being able to demonstrate the truly decrepit state of my dream house. All I kept thinking was how on Earth did the inspectors miss this? (By inspectors I mean my younger brother and his college roommate, Wally.)

My head was swimming. Hoot gave me a sideways glance; there was something else on his mind.

"So...," he chose his words very carefully. "You married?"

I quickly puffed up my chest and with the manliest bravado I could muster I squeaked out, "Naa... movin' up here with one of my buds."

Words cannot describe the look that suddenly washed over Hoot. Color drained from his face. He struggled to maintain his composure but inside he was screaming.

He knew.

I knew he knew.

And he knew I knew he knew.

The one guarantee about air mattresses is that they always end up with leaks. Wide awake in a fetal position I stared up at the cracks in the ceiling listening to a continuous "weeeeeeeeeeeeeee" as air streamed from some unseen pinhole. In about twenty minutes the mattress would be completely empty and I would be deposited flat on my back on beautiful hardwood floors throughout.

What was I thinking? Two queers buying a house in Dogpatch? Was I crazy? This is a disaster. So much for a sign from above. Thanks a lot, Dad.

The full moon filled the empty room with blue, underwater blue.

Rattlesnakes? That's ridiculous. This Hoot fellow is just being a jerk. There aren't any rattlesnakes up here! ...Are there?

"Weeeeeeeeeeeeeee...."

We're going to be murdered. He's going to take that knife and slit our throats in the middle of the night. I can see it now. Blood everywhere. I'm too young to die.

In the distance I could hear an owl.

"Hoot...hoot...hoot..."

How are we going to afford this dump? We don't even have jobs. Jobs? What jobs? There aren't any jobs up here. We can't go through with this. It's a mistake, a terrible awful mistake!

"Weeeeeeeeeeeeeee...."

And poor Vincent, on a red eye right now, winging across the country at thirty thousand feet completely unaware of the fact that our dream house is a nightmare.

"Hoot...Hoot...Hoot...."

I won't sign the papers. I haven't signed anything yet. Nobody can make me sign if I don't want to sign. I'll stand firm. I will march into Jeff Bank tomorrow morning and tell those suits and ties that there has been a change of plans and I am not going to sign those papers. I cannot sign. I will not sign!

"Weeeeeeeeeeeeeeee...."

They gave me a free pen and a really nice canvas tote with The First National Bank of Jeffersonville logo on the side. After the signing, I met up with Vincent at Ted's Restaurant and we had lunch to celebrate the start of an exciting new chapter in our lives.

I hardly touched any of my turkey club.

2.

Turns out we didn't get murdered right away.

As winter melted into spring we spent the days settling in. A mowed lawn, painted shutters and some Craigslist Adirondack chairs breathed new life into the orphaned farmstead. We bought twenty five baby chicks. Rhode Island Reds, Barred Rocks and Leghorns, the usual line up for future egg production. They arrived by United States Postal Service in a small cardboard box. Only one was dead, squished flat as a pancake by its box mates. All things considered, one dead chick out of twenty five isn't bad (unless you are that chick). We set up a brooder light in the reclaimed henhouse. From our bedroom window we could see the red glow in the night.

Of course everything was done under Hoot's watchful eye. For a guy who went unseen while we were first surveying the property, he now seemed to be ever present. Did he actually need to rake his front lawn and power-wash the siding on his trailer or was he just making up chores so that he could spy on the freak show next door?

For the most part we just went about our business. Hoot kept a safe distance but made sure we weren't breaking any mountain rules. Vincent playing show tunes with the windows open may have been a bit unsettling for poor Hoot. One particularly raucous rendition of *There's Nothin' Like A Dame* was more than Hoot could handle so he revved up his chainsaw and cut stuff.

Hoot was the Laurel Lane toll master, a self appointed position to which he had staked a claim long ago. No one got past Hoot without full examination, explanation and considerable exasperation. Jehovah help the unsuspecting Bible pusher who dare to peddle down this dirt trail.

Vincent, Poke and I were somehow granted free pass. Most of the time Hoot just gave us a small nod or a clipped wave but every once in a while he would purposely position himself so that we were obligated to stop the truck and chat. These conversations invariably began with Hoot saying, "I don't want to get in your business but...."

I do have to admit that as we became accustomed to mountain protocol, Hoot's presence became somehow almost comforting. Like a pit bull on a chain he kept the riff-raff away. I say chain because it turned out that Hoot had a wife, Stephanie. She was the principal of the local school. Stephanie mostly busied herself indoors making the LeShea trailer a home. In some way she also kept Hoot reined in.

But there would be no trouble on Hoot's watch. We became so lulled into a feeling of security that we soon stopped locking the front door. In fact at some point we misplaced the key altogether. Hoot assured us that if we ever happened to find ourselves locked out he would show us how to climb into our garage attic and drop down into the hall closet. The prospect was both comforting and disturbing.

Across the lane and over a sunny meadow was a pale yellow cottage with blue shutters. It was the home of an elderly couple named Ross and Viola Dink. Like two happy hobbits they doted on their yard and occasional visiting grandchildren. Viola welcomed us with a homemade gooseberry peanut butter pie.

Since Laurel Lane was a private road and therefore not maintained by the town or the county, old Ross took it upon himself to rake out the bumps and keep the ruts filled with gravel. Whereas Hoot was the gatekeeper, Ross was the groundskeeper. He spent many of his retirement hours keeping Laurel Lane as smooth and level as a Columbian air strip.

Ross was a sweet old guy, a bit hunched over, maybe from all that raking, but he was always happy to take a moment from his appointed chores to shoot the breeze. The first two things you noticed about Ross Dink was that; 1.) He was as blind as a sea sponge. And 2.) He always walked around with a Glock holstered to his belt (and by belt I mean piece of clothes line).

One day I was walking out to get the mail and I asked him, "Ross, why do you always carry that gun?"

He dapped at his watery eyes and squinted toward the woods.

"Coydogs," he bristled. "I got to protect myself from coydogs."

Coydogs are the legendary cross between feral dog and coyote. They roam the hills snarling and gnashing, preying on sheep and old men. The Catskill's own *chupacabra*, they are more myth than truth but don't tell that to Ross Dink and his Glock. From then on I made sure that Poke always wore a little bell.

Ross liked to reminisce about the good old days on the mountain, or as he called them, the salad days. Back when the mountain was a self sustained community and neighbors took care of neighbors.

His scratchy voice always sounded like he had a piece of toast stuck in his throat but his tales of days gone by were wonderful, how he and Viola first rolled up here in a borrowed Airstream and how with just an ax he cleared the woods. Ross built that cottage himself. At first it was just one room and an outhouse. He and Viola lived on a dirt floor for the first three years. The salad days always seemed to move Ross to tears. Or perhaps it was just his condition. I could never tell for sure.

Beyond our house Laurel Lane became more rutted as it dropped down into deep forest. I was told that there were a few inhabitants back there and an old abandoned hunting camp but I hadn't actually taken the time to venture any further. It seemed to me that some things were better left unexplored. Not to mention the fact that I didn't feel like getting harassed by any coydogs.

I soon settled into a nightly ritual, my constitutional, to walk the property and survey my kingdom, faithful dog at my side. Ours was a secluded world, cut off from neighbors and the rest of humankind by a wall of forsythia and lilac. A place where the sun set on an infinite expanse of woodland that radiated with a chorus of birdsong and the last of the day's light sparkled off the vast Neversink Reservoir. Spring in the Catskill Mountains is an unequaled heaven on earth.

Poke hurried between the lengthening shadows, sniffing out a cottontail that played a game of hide and seek with her. After a day of free ranging, the pullets had all gone up to roost. They were growing up fast. I closed the hen house door for the night.

These were probably the most peaceful moments in my life, watching as day dissolved into night. I felt invisible, listening to distant clunks as Hoot locked away his tools. He spoke softly with his wife then they went inside and closed the doors and turned off the outside light. Like a spirit in another dimension I looked back at our own home and through the glowing windows. Vincent didn't know I was watching as he poured himself another glass of wine.

Like the siren's song, cicadas and the gentle creatures of the night beckoned me to the edge of the forest. I made my way slowly into the woods to investigate a rustling sound. An evening warbler flipping leaves in search of grubs. Surprised by my presence, it flittered off into the darkness.

My dad always said that there are only two animals that tromp through the woods, elephants and humans. He taught us to learn from the deer and the wild turkey; take three gentle, thoughtful steps then pause, listen, observe, breathe slowly in and out, let the natural world flow through you, become one with the forest. Then take three more thoughtful steps and pause again.

I soon found myself deep in the forest, enveloped in dark, surrounded by a thousand fireflies and a billion stars above. It is a moment like this when one is aware of both eternity and mortality. Home was now just a tiny speck of light in a sea of black.

Then I heard a rustle of leaves. Was the warbler back or perhaps a deer?

"Poke?"

I called but she was nowhere. I stood motionless and just listened. Somewhere a twig snapped.

Then just over my left shoulder, in the darkness I heard a gentle yet terrifying sound.

A man cleared his throat.

I will tell you, I was no thoughtful deer when I ran out of that forest.

3.

One morning I was washing dishes when I heard the chickens making strange sounds, sounds that I had never heard them make before. I peered out the open kitchen window, squinting in the bright sunlight. At first I wasn't sure what I was seeing. The chickens had all gathered on the front lawn. They seemed agitated, bristling their feathers and clucking nervously. In a loose semicircle they surrounded a clump of branch that had fallen from the oak tree. At least that's what I thought it was. But as my eyes adjusted to the brightness and the branch came into focus, I suddenly realized that it was actually an enormous snake.

"Vincent!" I called out. "Vincent, come here quick!"

He could tell by my tone that something was urgent so he immediately came into the kitchen. I pointed outside. He looked out and I watched as his eyes adjusted to the sunlight and his expression changed from perplexed to astounded.

"Oh - my – god," he said.

I was wearing those big yellow dish washing gloves and I grabbed a spatula and headed for the door.

"Where are you going?!" Vincent shouted at me. "Stay inside!"

"I have to get a closer look."

I stepped out into the sunlight. Sensing my excitement Poke's hunting instincts kicked in and she followed me. Vincent called out from the front porch.

"Poke, get back here! Scott! Stay away from it!"

I cautiously approached the coiled reptile. It puffed up its body and released a rush of air. Its yellow eyes locked on Poke. Just a slight shake at first, like a toy maraca, but then it revved up and the snake's tail rattled with high voltage intensity.

"Poke. You stay back," I warned.

Her hair standing on end, her eyes fixed on the snake, she sniffed at the air and circled around. Something deep in her dog DNA told her to keep her distance. This was not a fluffy little bunny or some stupid squirrel. This was a very different creature.

"Scott, idiot, get back!" Vincent was freaked. "I swear!"

The rattling sound filled the air and the chickens backed away. Poke got behind me, not sure what to do. She quaked with nervous energy. The rattling slowed and the snake puffed its body again and flicked its forked tongue and for a moment I detected a strange aroma, thick, musky.

It was impossible for me to estimate the snake's length because it was coiled like a hose, folded neatly into itself. It was big for sure, meaty and thick. I know it's cliché to say, "as thick as a man's arm," but it was indeed as thick as a man's arm. Darker than I would have thought, with an incredible banding pattern down its back and that classic no-nonsense rattlesnake head. A living link to a prehistoric world, a scaly mass of muscle and venom. This was a dangerous animal. Incredible that nature designed a creature that can convert field mice into deadly poison.

Standing on the grass with my rubber gloves and spatula I suddenly realized that I was in my boxer shorts and bare feet.

"Get back here! *Please!*" Vincent hollered. Then he took out his phone and dialed 9-1-1.

There was little the 9-1-1 operator could do. It wasn't really an emergency since no one had actually been bitten. (Not yet anyway.) She switched Vincent over to the D.E.C., that's the Department of Environmental Conservation. Vincent spoke into the phone.

"Hi. I'm up on Laurel Lane. We have a rattlesnake here."

He switched to speaker phone but there was silence. Vincent scowled at me and waved his hand for me to come in then he spoke into the phone again.

"Hello...?"

The D.E.C. guy said, "Yes. Hello."

Vincent repeated, "We're up on Laurel Lane. We have a rattlesnake."

"You have a rattlesnake," the guy said. "A captured rattlesnake?"

Vincent clarified, "No, no. It's in our front yard."

The guy was quiet and then said, "Okay."

Vincent was befuddled. He glared at the phone.

"Well? Are you going to do something?!"

The guy asked, "Do what?"

At this point Vincent was exasperated.

"I don't know. Catch it?! Move it?! Kill it?!"

The guy spoke calmly and methodically, as if he were reading a prepared statement.

"Rattlesnakes are an endangered and protected species in New York State. They are not to be killed, captured, or relocated. They are not to be molested in any way. Keep a safe distance of at least fifteen feet away." He paused for a moment and then added, "Just leave it alone."

Vincent shouted, "But it's right outside my front door!"

The D.E.C. guy said, "So use your back door."

I don't know who hung up on whom.

I got Poke back into the house and locked her in a bedroom. She was barking and whining, beside herself with excitement. Vincent followed me to the laundry room where I pulled on a pair of rubber wading boots.

"What are you doing?!" he demanded. "Stay away from that thing!"

"We can't just leave it on our front lawn."

Vincent gave me a look and asked, *"Just what exactly are you planning to do?!"*

I looked at myself in the mirror and adjusted my rubber gloves.

"I don't know."

We went back to the kitchen to work out some sort of strategy. But when we looked out the window we saw something worse than a rattlesnake.

No rattlesnake.

"Shit!" Vincent said.

If it wasn't there, where was it?

Vincent and I tiptoed out onto the front lawn. I armed myself with a three prong garden rake and Vincent grabbed a straw broom and a thirty gallon garbage can. The grass had recently been mowed so it was cropped and open but there were certainly places for a snake to hide. There were shrubs and flowers, and the front porch. Don't forget the front porch, dark and shady under there. That snake could be anywhere, including right under our feet.

I held my breath as I used the prong end of the rake to push aside a juniper bough.

Nothing.

I flipped over some leaves and poked between the flowers.

Nothing.

Vincent was right at my side, ready to jump backwards if necessary.

He whispered, "Maybe it went back into the woods."

I whispered, "But we weren't in the house that long."

He whispered, "Maybe it went down a hole."

I whispered, "What hole?"

He whispered, "There must be a hole."

I whispered, "Why are we whispering?"

He whispered, "I don't know. Can snakes hear?"

I whispered, "I think with their tongues,"

Finally, Vincent decided he had to do what he had to do. He stood the garbage can off to one side, leaned the broom against it and slowly, ever so slowly, he got down on all fours, put his face at ground level and peered underneath the porch. He breathed in through his nose and calmly exhaled.

"Well helloooo, Mama."

Before Vincent and I had a chance to formulate a workable plan we heard the droning of an engine and Hoot came bouncing up the road on his ATV. After a long day of logging deep in the forest he was surely tired and anxious to get home to his sweet wife but the sight of his two knucklehead neighbors in rubber boots and rubber gloves wielding a broom and a rake demanded his immediate attention. Vincent waved him in and Hoot rolled to a stop on the front lawn and cut the engine.

Vincent pointed to the porch and said, "Snake."

Intrigued, Hoot dismounted and approached us without saying a word. He narrowed his eyes, unsure of what to make of our curious attire. Vincent motioned for Hoot to have a look for himself. Hoot walked over to the porch, dropped down onto the grass and peered under. He said nothing, just took a moment to allow his eyes to adjust to the shadows and assess the situation. Then he stood up straight, stepped back, and brushed bits of grass off his shirt.

"That is one big snake."

"So what do we do?" I said. "It can't stay here. Poke needs to go out and we have to..."

"Hang on, hang on. Let me think about this."

With one hand Hoot lifted his hat and scratched the top of his head.

"Okay, you got that garbage can and that broom." Hoot paced back and forth along the front of the porch. "Gimme that rake."

I handed Hoot the rake. He flipped it back and forth, feeling its weight, calculating its capabilities. Then he dropped back down onto his belly and disappeared halfway under the porch. Only his legs were sticking out. Suddenly the air reverberated with the throbbing buzz of an angry rattlesnake.

"What's going on?!" I hollered.

Hoot didn't answer but we could see him moving and twisting his body to get into a better position. In a jolt the snake appeared from under the front steps and rippled out onto the driveway.

"There it is!" Vincent shouted. "It's huge!"

The snake huffed and spit and bundled itself back into a writhing coil once again. The rattling intensified, even louder than before. Hoot leapt around to block its path back to the porch.

"Drop the garbage can!" he shouted. "Here! Over here!"

Vincent dropped the garbage can onto its side and held the broom in both hands like a goalie with a hockey stick. It was only then that I noticed he was wearing flip flops.

Hoot gently nudged the snake with the prongs of the rake and it lunged forward and sunk its fangs into the wooden handle. Hoot dropped the rake and jumped back like a Ninja. I shrieked like a stepped-on mouse. Hoot scooted forward and reclaimed the rake. The snake slithered to the left. Vincent cut off its path with the broom. It opened its mouth and flashed its gleaming fangs. It hissed and then tried to escape to the right. Hoot blocked it with the rake. It veered to the left again. With the heel of his flip flop, Vincent kicked at the garbage can rolling it directly into the path of the snake. The snake took final desperate refuge in the garbage can. Instantly and in one graceful motion, Hoot leapt forward and with the very tips of just two fingers he flipped the garbage can into an upright position and the snake slumped to the bottom.

In true hillbilly style the three of us jumped and hooted and high fived each other.

"That was intense!" Vincent exclaimed.

"Big boy!" Hoot said. "Biggest I've seen! I told ya's! Didn't I tell ya?! I told ya they were here!"

I had goose bumps. Grinning from ear to ear, I was caught up in the excitement of the moment.

"I can't believe we-" I stopped midsentence and shouted, "Oh no!"

Like a snake charmer's cobra, the rattlesnake raised itself along the inside of the garbage can, stretching so that its head was now peeking over the rim.

I grabbed a nearby lid and handed it off to Vincent who Frisbeed it to Hoot who then sprung forward and quickly slammed it onto the top of the garbage can. Hoot held it in place with both hands and turned toward us with a look of absolute exasperation.

"Shew!" he exhaled. "Feisty bastard."

Six bungee cords and half a roll of duct tape later we all felt confident that the lid and the snake were finally secure. We tied the garbage can onto the back of Hoot's ATV. He climbed into the seat and turned the key. Hoot's back was flat up against the garbage can. He and the snake were separated by mere millimeters of molded plastic but Hoot was calm and composed, quite proud of himself.

I saw a different side to Hoot that day. Here was this deer-hunting, coon-trapping woodsman and yet he had no intention of harming that snake. He valued its place in the natural world.

With a crank of the handlebar, Hoot revved the engine. He would find another rocky, south facing slope far back in the hills and there he would release our snake to live out its days unmolested by man in one of the last of the wild places.

Hoot smirked at me and Vincent.

"Never a dull moment with you boys, never a dull moment."

The tires tore a patch in the lawn as his ATV peeled away down Laurel Lane and up the old logging trail.

4.

I was a bit stunned when I entered the chicken coop one morning and discovered the lifeless body of a headless chicken on the floor. There were little bloody paw prints left by some unidentified predator that had accessed a broken window.

I didn't know how I was going to tell Vincent. Some people think it's bad luck to name your chickens. This happened to be one chicken that Vincent had named, Ruby, after his fourth grade teacher Mrs. Ruby who, like the chicken, was quite buxom. Booby Ruby he called them both.

I picked up the poor deceased bird by her legs. I was surprised how heavy she was. Her feathers were shiny and beautiful. She was really quite a fine specimen, except for the missing head. The other chickens seemed only mildly upset at Ruby's untimely demise. They were more concerned with when I planned to toss them some scratch grain. That's the thing about chickens: they don't dwell on the past.

Suddenly Hoot appeared at the window. He frowned at the sight of me standing there holding a dead chicken.

"Ut oh," he said.

Then like a forensic detective, he scrutinized the bloody prints on the window sill.

"That's a mink. You got a mink. Better fix this window. He'll be back for sure."

I just sighed.

Hoot walked around the front and came into the coop.

"Yep. Mink will eat the head right off and suck out the blood. Got to fix that window." Then he nodded toward the dead hen and said, "Oh well, never have a pet you can't eat."

I told Hoot about my experience in the woods a few nights back. I was sure I heard a man clear his throat. Hoot pondered it for a moment.

"Ay- that's just Psycho Pete the taxidermist."

"Taxidermist?" (I completely glossed over the word "psycho".)

"Sure," said Hoot. "He likes to walk around in the woods."

Then he added, "at night."

Then he added, "naked."

I frowned. Surely Hoot was embellishing. But then I remembered that I had also doubted his rattlesnake accounts.

"He's harmless," Hoot said. "Lives down in town."

I was trying to digest the dynamics of having a crazy naked taxidermist running around in the forest when Hoot changed the subject.

"I don't want to get in your business but...," he began. "You need to hire my nephew to work for you."

I kind of chuckled. What was he talking about? We weren't hiring anybody for anything. I didn't even have a job myself. Vincent had just been hired and was about to start training to become a flight attendant but that was still weeks away and at this point we were barely able to pay for chicken feed.

Ever the salesman Hoot tried to sweeten the deal.

"My nephew's a bum. Gets involved with those idiots up the hill. I don't know if you read the papers." He shook his head. "Quit school and now this shit. The kid needs a job. He's a real bum."

He sounds perfect. Have him fill out an application.

"Yeah well, Hoot...," I tried to be tactful. "I'll keep him in mind. But we really don't need anything at this time."

"What are you kidding me? This place is a dump." Hoot always knew just what to say. "The kid can paint the siding and cut the lawn. I'll tell him to stop over in the morning." Then he smirked. "He can help you fix those rotten beams."

"Yes but we can't hire anybody."

I tried but in Hoot's mind the deal was sealed.

"I'll send him over," he said. Then he looked at Ruby. "You gonna eat that?"

38

That evening Vincent and I relaxed on the back deck sipping wine, listening to crickets and enjoying our little domain. Vincent seemed so content. I just sat there, my thoughts churning. I didn't bother mentioning Hoot stopping over or Psycho Pete or headless Booby Ruby. It was all just too complicated and I didn't want to spoil the moment.

Poke was sitting out at the edge of the lawn, staring down into the dark woods. Vincent called to her.

"What do you see, girl? You smell something? Deer?" He turned to me. "You never know what creatures are lurking around out there."

I just sat there with a worried grin plastered to my face. I felt like a cement statue. Vincent took a sip of wine and stretched out on the chaise lounge.

"Ah... this is the life." Then he clinked his glass against mine. "Here's to our beautiful home."

A savory aroma drifted on the warm evening breeze.

"Mm... smell that?" Vincent said. "I think ol' Hoot's barbequing something."

I didn't have the heart to tell him it was Ruby.

The next morning we woke to birds singing and sunlight sparkling through the plantation shutters. All my troubles seem to have melted away with the morning light. They always do.

Why do I worry so much? Seriously, there is something wrong with me.

Vincent climbed out of bed, stretched and scratched himself, ready to seize the day. He looked out through the shutters.

"Hey... there's some kid out there."

"What?!" I jumped out of bed and pulled on yesterday's jeans. "He actually showed up?"

I stumbled around looking for a T-shirt, peeking out the window. A tall lanky kid, probably in his late teens, was sitting on the picnic table.

"Who is he?" Vincent asked. "What's he doing here?"

"It's Hoot's cousin, or nephew," I said. "He's looking for a job. Why can't I ever find two socks that match?"

I marched across the lawn with Poke bounding out ahead of me.

"Hey. How you doing? You're Hoot's nephew."

The kid stood up and wiped his hands on his pants.

"Yeah, Neil," he said as we sort of shook hands.

"Look, I told Hoot," I tried to let him down easy. "We really don't need anyone."

"Yeah, Uncle Hoot told me your place was a real dump. I'll help you get it fixed up."

"Thank you. I mean... we're really not hiring anyone."

"No worries. I'll just do whatever." He picked up a rake that was leaning against a tree and started raking.

"No, but wait...," I stopped him. "Like I was telling Hoot...."

Vincent came out onto the deck. The two exchanged "Heys".

"Why don't you have him start by putting those shingles on the shed roof?"

The kid dropped the rake.

"I get to climb on the roof?"

I felt like I was losing control.

"Nobody's climbing on the roof," I assured him.

"You got a hammer?" he asked.

"Wait a second...guys... Vincent!" No one was listening to me. "We can't pay...."

"I get five bucks an hour."

"Great," Vincent said. "The ladder's in the shed. And hammers and shingles too."

I was about to intervene when I thought, only five bucks an hour?

Neil was seventeen years old. He quit school because "them idiots don't know nothin'," and because "I could learn more from a school of bullheads." He had a shock of blond hair that looked like it had been cut with a sickle and straight white teeth but a crooked smile. He was all angular and gawky yet somehow good looking, in that backwoods sort of way. He wore duct tape around his boots to keep the soles on. He may not have been schooled but he sure knew everything.

For example: "I hate this daylights saving thing because you change the clocks back and it screws up all the animals. Like the raccoons are coming out in the morning and the roosters are crowing in the middle of the night."

And then there was: "If moths are attracted to light, why don't they just come out in the daytime?"

And his classic: "Sure a dog can be half beagle and half dachshund and half lab. It just has to be a really long dog."

Neil and I worked all day on the roof and I have to say that it came out great and I may not have gotten it done without him. Well, I would have but it would have taken me longer and it wouldn't have been half as entertaining. At five bucks an hour, how could we afford not to have a servant? He cleaned out the chicken coop and the gutters on the house. I had him mow the lawn and rake the driveway. I have to admit, in no time at all the old dump was starting to look pretty ritzy.

Neil really got into power-washing Rusty, scouring off all the rust to a point where I actually had to stop him or I would have ended up driving around on nothing more than a chassis.

I got the feeling that he didn't have any other place to go. Every morning he was outside waiting on the picnic table. This was like his new hang out.

I wondered what he thought about Vincent and me. He was very friendly toward both of us so I assumed it didn't faze him. But it was never openly discussed.

There was one time Neil told me he had been chatting with this really hot girl that he met on the internet. They had been sexting every night. I laughed.

"You do realize that you are probably conversing with a bald, fat, middle-aged man?"

Neil flashed his crooked smile.

"I don't go that way. Anyways, she's hot."

Oh and another classic Neil: He didn't think he would ever be able to meet this girl because "she lives in New Mexico and I don't ever plan to leave the good old U. S. of A.".

I showed Neil a bunch of power tools and old boards that had been left behind in the tool shed. I asked him if he could maybe build us a toilet paper holder. The one in our bathroom was ceramic and only held the small economy rolls. We constantly had to replace them.

Neil dove into that project. I could hear him sawing and hammering and drilling. It sounded like Santa's Workshop on December 23rd. I started thinking the kid may have found his calling.

While Neil was busy with that I went out and put together a little art studio in the shed. I swept it out and set up my easel and chair. It was really pretty nice. Except for the bees.

Later when I went to check on Neil, he very proudly showed off this insane contraption that he built into the bathroom wall. It looked like a giant Pez dispenser. It held ten rolls of toilet paper at once. It was, without a doubt, the most ridiculous thing I had ever seen.

And it works great. We almost never run out of toilet paper.

You have to get one.

5.

Just your typical January night in the Catskills, even though it was only November.

A thick layer of wet snow was on the ground with steady sleet pelting down like gravel and then turning to rain, then to snow, then back to sleet again.

Vincent was away at flight attendant boot camp. (Yes, there is such a place.) Poke and I had settled in for a long winter's night. We couldn't go anywhere if we wanted to and no one could get to us. We had everything we needed.

I was wearing my fuzzy pajama pants and had just poured a glass of Cabernet. Miraculously, the satellite was still working. I was taking advantage of the internet while I could. Poke was in the living room asleep on the couch with the TV blaring. It was blissful, really. Until... a strange feeling began to creep into my consciousness, like I was awakening from a dream.

At first I couldn't put my finger on it, but something was not quite right. In the other room the TV was yammering away but I hadn't really been paying attention to it. I don't even know what show was on but someone kept saying, "Help me.... Help me...." I paused my computer and sat up straight to listen. "Someone please... help me," said a voice, raspy and hoarse. *That was on the television, right?* It was difficult to hear over the driving sleet on the roof.

But I'll tell you when it got really freaky. A commercial for Viagra came on and yet there it was again.

"Help me."

Perhaps a man who needs Viagra would be crying for help but, seriously?

I slowly got up and tiptoed across the room, turning off the lights, cowering in the shadows. I listened. If it wasn't on television, if it was a person, surely Poke would have barked. I got down low and slinked into the living room, shutting off more lights. My heart was pounding and my hand trembled as I reached for the TV remote. I hit the mute button. And waited.

And there it was.

"Help me! Please help me!"

Poke leapt up and barked into action. The curtains were drawn. I couldn't see a thing. But I heard it for sure, a person, just outside the window, now tapping on the glass.

At this point Poke was ballistic. Between her barking and the sleet I couldn't think straight. I grabbed Poke by the collar and sequestered her in a bedroom. I squeezed myself into a corner wall. I could see my cell phone on the table in the living room but I was trembling in my fuzzy pajamas and couldn't move.

Who would be out on a night like this?! It had to be Psycho Pete. Maybe it was a trick. Someone was trying to get me to open the door. Maybe it was people from up the hill. I don't know who lives back there. Could be drug addicts. Maybe they have a meth lab. Could be Satan worshippers or cult members.

48

They heard about us moving here, two gay guys. They think we have money.

Now the ice turned back to snow and everything fell silent. Terrifyingly silent. There was no choice; I had to go for it. Like a raccoon, I scurried across the floor in the darkness and grabbed the phone.

My trembling fingers stabbed out 9-1-1. I had never dialed 9-1-1 before. I felt like I was in a movie.

"Nine-one-one operator, what's your emergency?"

I could barely choke out the words.

"Someone...is outside...my house."

"Sir? What are you saying? You have an intruder?"

"I think...it might be...Psycho Pete."

"Can you repeat that sir?"

"The taxidermist," I clarified.

I was crouched up against the back of the couch as I tried to explain my situation to the operator. The biggest challenge was trying to tell her exactly where I lived. When the operator thought she had figured out my location she groaned.

"You know the roads are horrible. Completely iced. I'm sending someone but they may have to go way around. You're just going to have to hold your horses."

I scanned the room for a weapon and finally settled on a twelve inch tall replica of a Chinese terracotta warrior. I grabbed him by the head and held tight. I told the operator that I was going to hang up and call my neighbor. Ten thirty at night, I was about ready to go to bed and here I was calling the neighbor. Keeping the warrior at the ready, I dialed with my thumb.

Hoot sounded like he just woke up.

"Hello?"

"Hoot. It's your neighbor. It's Scott. Sorry to call so late..."

"Everything okay?"

"Somebody is outside my house. Somebody's saying *Help me. Help me.*"

Silence then, "You shittin' me?"

"Hoot, I swear to God! Right outside my window!"

Within minutes Hoot was banging on the front door. I don't think he even hung up the phone.

"It's me! It's Hoot! Open the door!"

I flicked on the outside light and opened the door. Hoot was ready for action, armed with a twelve gauge shot gun. He was wearing big rubber galoshes, thermal long johns, a bulky hunting jacket with the game tag still pinned to the back and, of course, his flap-eared hat.

"You better not be shittin' me."

"I swear Hoot. I heard it," I said. "Look there – footprints!"

I pointed to fresh tracks in the snow along the front side of the house. Hoot cocked his gun and scanned the dark. Then we noticed a single wet bare footprint on the porch. Like a Native American on a bison hunt, Hoot crouched down to examine the print. I whispered to him.

"Psycho Pete?"

Before Hoot could answer I caught sight of a person sitting in the passenger seat of my truck parked in the driveway.

"Hoot look!"

Hoot swung around and aimed the gun at the cold white face staring back at us through a steamed-up window.

"Come out with your hands up!"

I swear he really said that.

The face in the window blinked and then slowly the truck door opened.

It was a woman in her late thirties, plump and red cheeked and soaking wet. Her glazed eyes stared out from behind stringy wet hair that hung down like tentacles over her face.

"Hoot," she gasped.

Then she half slid and half belly flopped face down onto the slush covered driveway. She flailed about like a baby sea turtle struggling to get to the ocean.

"Jesus Christ," Hoot exclaimed. "It's Drunk Again Louise."

Allow me a moment to introduce. As her title so aptly suggests, Drunk Again Louise is a local girl who likes to stay well lubricated. She lives a stumble or two down the lane with her husband, Quinn, in a chaotic trailer that looks as if it had been dropped there by a tornado. Quinn is a hermit and Louise is not just his soul mate but also his connection to the outside world. She had, on one or two occasions, staggered by our happy home, but Hoot always kept her moving along using every means possible, short of a cattle prod. Louise lost her driving privileges long ago. Not because of any police summons, though there had been a few, but because one night returning home from a bender she parked her '92 Civic so tightly between two trees that Quinn could only extract Louise by removing the back window. The Honda is now a permanent art installation just off in the woods halfway down the lane.

But what would bring Louise out on a night like this?

"I was downtown partying with Terry, Booger and Joey T..." (Ah, there's your answer.) "I hitchhiked home but the dirtballs wouldn't drive me up the mountain cause the roads are all icy."

Hoot held the gun to one side and leaned down to reach under her arm in an attempt to lift her off the ground. It was like trying to lift a soaking wet futon mattress. She was wearing only one shoe that was half hanging off and the other foot was bare except for a pink sock that was dangling from her big toe like a spent condom. She screamed in agony as Hoot tried unsuccessfully to right her.

"I broke my foot!"

That's when I realized that her shoe wasn't half off, her foot was. It was literally cracked at a right angle to her leg. I thought I was going to vomit.

Hoot glared up at me.

"We have to bring her into your house!"

Is he talking to me? I'm in my fuzzy pajamas. I'm about to have a cup of warm milk with a teaspoon of maple syrup and snuggle in bed with Poke and the latest issue of Chicken Fancy.

"But...but...but...." There had to be a way out of this. "But... why don't we bring her to your house?" I so gallantly offered.

Hoot's jaw dropped.

"My house?!" he gasped, losing his grip on the sack of Louise. *"It's way up the road!"* he said with a look of complete desperation.

My visions of warm milk soured.

"Bring her in."

Outside, flashing lights from three state trooper vehicles and an ambulance lit up the bare trees like a forest discotheque. Drunk Again Louise sat on a stool in my kitchen, surrounded by a squad of troopers and medics. She sobbed about her woes to anyone who would listen. Snot ran down her pudgy face and water puddled on the kitchen floor beneath her. I offered Louise one of Poke's blankets. I wasn't about to hand over one of our good blankets, we'd never see it again. Besides, I figured right now a few dog hairs were the least of her problems.

"I tried to find my way up through the woods but I got lost," she explained.

Keep in mind that the woods between our house and the road to town are a steep, dark, boulder-strewn primordial forest, tangled with ice coated roots, vines and fallen trees.

Difficult to navigate on a summer afternoon, never mind tonight.

"I slipped on a rock and heard my foot break. I crawled toward the light. And it was your house."

Four state troopers, three paramedics and Hoot were all tending to Louise who just sat there sobbing. My quiet little sanctuary in the hills was now a fully staffed emergency room. Poke even joined the festivities, wiggling and wagging between everyone like she was the hostess at a cocktail party. In fact at one point I passed around an open bag of Doritos.

Louise winced in pain as a paramedic strapped her broken ankle into a temporary splint. It was like Cinderella being fitted with the glass slipper by her prince. Only not. She looked up at me through weepy eyes.

"I'm sorry I got in your truck. I would never do that 'cept I thought I was going to die. I rung the doorbell like a hundred times but you wouldn't answer."

Everyone looked at me. I sort of smiled and sort of shrugged.

I have got to fix that stupid doorbell.

Vincent was not going to believe what he missed. I decided to document everything with my camera. I was focusing on a group shot when I noticed a thin man with a long white ZZ Top beard peek in from around the corner. He looked like a wizard or Rip Van Winkle, neither of which would have surprised me at this point.

Turned out it was Louise's husband, Quinn, who had been alerted to all the commotion by his police scanner. He politely introduced himself and apologized for us having to meet under such extraordinary circumstances and thanked me for being so neighborly. I assured him, it was the least I could do.

Quinn is soft spoken and he's fascinating once you get to know him. He moved back here seventeen years ago. He weaves baskets out of wild grape vines, collects and dries unusually shaped mushrooms that resemble historic figures, makes his own birch beer and is a Harvard graduate with a PhD in International Business Law.

As Louise was hoisted onto a gurney she wailed, "I'm sorry Hoot!"

Hoot patted her on the head like she was a wet puppy.

"Don't worry about it," he said.

She blushed and smiled up at him, pleased that The Mayor had forgiven her. The men struggled to wedge the stretcher out the front door. When the gurney bumped against the porch railing, Louise writhed in pain and sobbed.

"I'm a Brooklyn girl! This isn't supposed to happen to me!"

The entire party escorted her out to the waiting ambulance. Like the Queen, Louise held up a hand and waved to show that she was going to be fine.

Sirens blaring and lights whirling, Louise was crated up and hauled away. The ambulance and trooper trucks rumbled down Laurel Lane, disappearing into the night.

The sleet had turned to snow again. Hoot slung the rifle over one shoulder and tugged down on his flap-eared hat.

"Dirty night."

Then he too disappeared into the darkness. Poke and I went back into the house and I put a cup of milk with a teaspoon of syrup into the microwave.

It turns out that Louise actually did suffer a compound fracture of the lower tibia. She spent several months in rehab for her bone and her sobriety. I am happy to report that she is doing much better with both. She now spends her days quietly tending her garden.

One morning some months after that fitful night we discovered a lovely grapevine basket on our doorstep. Inside was a sweet note from Louise along with some garden fresh rhubarb, several bottles of homemade birch beer and Poke's blanket, washed and neatly folded, not a dog hair to be found.

6.

Hoot sold me a trailer load of firewood. Good stuff too, a full generous cord and the bark was falling off which meant it was well seasoned. Of course I growled about the price, one seventy five, which I actually thought was a pretty good price, but being schooled in the language of the hills I knew it was customary to growl. Hoot growled right back.

I had to grab my keys and move my truck so that Hoot could back his big diesel beast into the yard and dump the load of wood. Poke was running around between the trucks and the trailer wanting to be part of the excitement.

"Get back dog!" I said. She knew to stay out of the way.

It was really impressive how Hoot could maneuver the trailer between walls of plowed snow. He climbed out of the cab and lifted a big battery from the back of his truck and hooked it up to two wire cables that hung between the hitch and the trailer. A small winch began to whine and the bed of the trailer lifted at one end and dumped the heavy load down onto the frozen ground. The blocks of split wood clunked like bowling pins.

"That'll get you through the weekend," Hoot scoffed.

"I don't know. Doesn't look like a full cord to me," I scoffed back.

"Ha! It's a cord plus, and you're still gonna need more." Hoot studied the sky. "This winter ain't over yet."

I knew he was right. Between firewood, propane and electricity, a Catskill winter can be a very pricey undertaking.

"This'll be my eighty-seventh load I done so far this year," Hoot said as the now empty bed of the trailer whined its way back down. "My brother and me one year did two hundred and twenty-two loads. Two two two, that was our goal and we did it, just him and me alone."

Snow was collecting in Hoot's goatee.

"We made a lot of money. That was a good winter."

He yanked the cables free and hefted the big battery back to his truck.

"Anyway, now he's dead."

I didn't know what to say. I stuck my hands into my coat pockets.

"Oh yeah," I said. "Sorry. I heard you had a brother."

Hoot had mentioned it once in passing and Ross had said something but I didn't know the details. I honestly didn't want to ask. It was really cold and I was wearing my slippers. Right now I just wanted my load of firewood and to get back into the warm house. Hoot opened the door to the truck.

"No matter," he said.

Then suddenly words just popped out of my mouth. I couldn't help it.

"How did your brother die?"

Hoot stopped. He stared at the snow falling into the open cab.

"Tree."

I nodded but said nothing. I wasn't sure what he meant but I was reluctant to pry any further. I figured it was up to Hoot if he wanted to say more. And he did.

"He was cutting down a tree."

Hoot removed his gloves and used them to brush snow off the driver's seat.

"He would be thirty. That was eight years ago. Eight years and I still think about it every day."

The seat was clean but Hoot kept brushing.

"I never should have run up there. In the woods by Baker Falls. Big hemlock, probably three tons, it crushed him to the ground." Hoot shook his head in disgust. "He got gypped."

I nodded. There was no denying.

"The troopers tried to hold me back, but I pushed through. I wish I didn't but I did."

This was the most I ever heard Hoot say. It seemed like he had to say it so I just stood there and let him.

"They had a canvas over him but I could see his boots." Hoot shook his head from side to side. "I can't get those boots out of my mind."

"But Hoot," I said quickly, desperately. "Don't think about that."

Hoot stared at the truck seat.

"Can't help it."

"You got to try," I said. "That was just one tiny part of his whole life. Think of all the good things about your brother." Hoot nodded.

"He was a good kid, a great kid, worked hard every day. Not like some of these freeloaders," he motioned toward the back hills. Then he looked over at the wood pile. "I'm only doing this for him, you know. To keep him going somehow. He loved doing firewood. We both did."

"That's good," I said. Hoot smiled.

"I still use his old chainsaw. I put over a grand into that thing but I don't care. I keep it going."

"Your brother wouldn't want you to be unhappy," I offered though it seemed pale. "You're doing great. Keep doing great. Make something positive come of it."

Hoot sort of shrugged.

"I don't drink no more," he said. "Never again since that day."

"That would make him proud."

I didn't want to get too mushy or anything. You don't get mushy up here in the mountains. Plus my feet were freezing and I really didn't want to get into it. I really didn't.

But then I did.

"You know, Hoot, I also had a brother who died."

Hoot looked up and for the first time looked straight into my eyes.

"Tree?"

"No," I sort of smiled. "He had a kidney disease. He was born with it. But he never seemed sick or anything. I mean he was a robust little kid. You would never know anything was really wrong. Until he died."

Hoot just listened.

"We were four brothers and now we are three. I always felt bad too, because I teased him. We were just kids. I didn't know anything was going to happen. The last memory I have of my little brother and I was being mean to him. All these years later and I still feel bad about it."

Hoot clenched his jaw and took a deep breath.

"Don't beat yourself up. That's just what kids do. You gotta remember the good things."

"I do," I said. "Of course I do."

There was a weird moment when Hoot and I were just thinking and not talking.

"I always try to never be mean to anyone," I said, "in honor of my brother. I just try to be good to people because... you never know."

Hoot agreed.

"You never know."

It was snowing really hard now and it turned out that I had backed my truck into a snow bank and it was stuck. Even in four wheel drive I couldn't get it out. We had to hook a big chain to Little Rusty and Hoot towed him out with The Beast.

"You flatlanders don't know how to drive in the snow," Hoot grumbled as he unhooked the chain. He stood up and shook the snow off his back.

"You hillbillies don't know what a full cord of wood looks like," I replied.

Then we both got into our trucks and drove off with a *toot-toot* of the horns.

We never spoke of our brothers again.

7.

It's so exciting to see a celebrity in our neck of the woods.

You'd be surprised though, a lot of famous people seek the solitude and own second homes up here. One afternoon I was thrilled to spot Otis Nolan in Jeff Bank. I swear, Otis Nolan! Just standing in line like everybody else.

For the few of you who may not know who he is, Otis Nolan is a world class giant pumpkin grower who was featured in the much acclaimed documentary *Grow Big*. And now here he was right in front of me waiting for a teller just like a regular person!

Hoping to get his attention I cleared my throat. When that didn't work I made like I was reaching for a deposit slip and then accidentally on purpose I bumped him.

"Oops," I said. "Excuse me."

You should have seen the good acting job I did pretending to be surprised.

"Oh, Mr. Nolan," I said. "You're Otis Nolan."

He eyed me suspiciously. (I'm sure he gets this sort of thing all the time.)

I smiled politely. I didn't want him to think I was some crazed stalker.

"My name is Scott Woods. I've seen your pumpkins."

That didn't come out right.

"I mean on TV," I quickly added. "I've seen *Grow Big*, like, four times."

He sort of smiled but said nothing. I tried to keep the conversation going.

"I'm a bit of a gardener myself," I added.

Otis grunted in acknowledgement then quickly stepped up to the teller's window. I sounded so pathetic. Imagine me telling Otis Nolan that I was a bit of a gardener. As if.

But much to my surprise when Otis finished his transaction he turned to me.

"You grow the big punkins?"

I stared down at my shoes.

"Well... not as big as yours," I said. Then I looked up and smiled. "But I do love to grow things and I am pretty darn good at it."

Otis studied me. He's a tall guy with glasses, a bushy mustache and a permanent baseball cap.

"Tell you what," he said, grabbing a pencil stub from behind his ear. "I got some baby plants, from Pacific Giants. Record breakers. Thousand-pound mother."

He jotted something down on the back of a deposit slip.

"Meet me at my house, one hour from now and I'll give you one."

World champion pumpkin grower Otis Nolan was going to give little old me one of his babies. Such an honor! I was sure everyone in the bank was eyeing me with envy. I tucked his address into my pocket and followed Mr. Nolan to the door like a cocker spaniel. He smiled and held the door open for me. It felt as if I was stepping out of Jeff Bank and into the Eternal Order of World Class Giant Pumpkin Growers. Yes, I was a personal friend of Otis Nolan and that's right, I was going to be raising one of his babies.

We shook hands and I climbed into my little truck. I was charged with enthusiasm, thrilled to be embarking on the beginning of a beautiful relationship.

Let me tell you something right now. It did not end well.

One hour later, having changed into a crisp new shirt and carrying a dozen fresh eggs from our hens (you know, as a token of my appreciation), I arrived at the Nolan residence. It's a curiously humble house, not as grand as one would have expected for a celebrity. There was a miniature windmill next to a miniature fishpond and a miniature sign that read "No Fishing," even though there was a statue of a miniature boy who was indeed fishing. The irony, I couldn't help but smile.

71

A paved walk led straight to the front door. The place was as neat as a pin. Meticulous garden beds with razor straight edges surrounded the yard. Vines were staked on measured poles and wire fencing as tight as harp strings. Every plant was properly spaced and perfectly pruned and not a weed, not a weed to be seen. It all seemed to teeter between very organized and obsessive compulsive.

Then I caught sight of Otis standing tall behind the glass of a front bay window. He motioned for me to stop right where I was. I waited for further instruction. He pointed down. There on the step was a single three leaf plant in a little peat pot.

I looked up at Otis. He stood proud. I held up the carton of eggs. Otis nodded his divine approval. I placed the eggs on the step and very carefully lifted up the little plant, hoping Otis would notice that I was a devoted parent.

The little plant seemed almost iridescent green, a healthier seedling you have never seen and never will. I cradled it to my chest and looked up in appreciation but Mr. Nolan was gone. I stood alone with my adopted child.

With the utmost care I planted my baby in a sunny corner of our garden just to the left of the compost pile. I figured any compost run-off would surely be good for a young pumpkin vine. It looked happy. Everything was going to be just fine.

About a week or so later I bumped into Otis Nolan again, this time at the post office. When he saw me he recognized me right away. I felt so worthy. He sort of lit up.

"Well hi there Steve," he said. "How's that punkin doing?"

Now just between you and me I hadn't really had a chance to look at it since I had first planted it. It happened to be a particularly busy couple of weeks. I had to run down to Jersey and then we had that problem with our septic. There never seemed to be enough time. So of course I lied.

"Oh good good, real good, doubled in size already."

Wait a second, did he call me Steve?

Otis stared at me.

"You giving it electrolytes?"

Was I supposed to be? Where does one get electrolytes?

"I crush up egg shells," he said. "Young punkins need calcium."

I nodded knowingly.

"And milk," he added. "Quarter cup of milk twice a day."

Milk? Am I raising a pumpkin or a chimp? I struggled to sound informed.

"I planted it next to the compost pile."

Otis scrunched his mustache to one side.

"What's your soil pH? You got to have the proper pH."

In the first place, I haven't the foggiest idea what my pH is. What is it supposed to be? For that matter, what does pH really even mean? I feigned confidence.

"Oh, it's good. Real good pH."

Otis gave me a funny look. I pretended I was checking my mail. I was pretty sure I had dodged that one, for the moment anyway. But just as I was about to turn and slip away Otis dropped a bomb.

"I'll stop over one day."

I drove home in a panic.

Stop over? Did he really say that? He wouldn't really just stop over would he? What is he, social services? What have I signed up for here? I just thought it would be fun to grow a giant pumpkin. I didn't know there were going to be pop quizzes. He doesn't know where I live, does he? I better check the pH. What is proper pumpkin pH anyway? Where do I get electrolytes? He couldn't possibly know where I live.

As soon as I got home I poured a cup of milk and headed for the garden. Milk dripping down my arm I hurried past Vincent on the back deck. He looked puzzled.

"What are you up to?"

No time. No time to chit chat. Vincent just shook his head.

I hacked my way through the garden. Now where was that pumpkin plant? The weeds were certainly thriving. Two weeks and the place had turned into the jungles of Vietnam.

Finally I spotted the little demon seed. And I have to tell you he wasn't looking too happy. It certainly hadn't doubled in size as I had so smugly boasted. In fact I don't think it had grown at all. Wait a second... could it actually have shrunk a bit? Is that possible? Can a plant grow smaller?

I kneeled down for a closer look. It definitely wasn't that healthy green anymore. In fact one leaf looked sort of yellow and limp. And spots. What were those spots?!

I poured the milk around the plant, a full cup. And whole milk not 2%. No more fooling around. We had to make up for lost time. I pulled a few weeds out of the way and in doing so I accidently broke the yellow leaf clean off.

I made a feeble attempt to put the leaf back on but that was obviously ridiculous so I hid it under a bucket. Without the yellow leaf the plant was now even smaller. I stood up to walk away but then I had to look back. Maybe it wasn't as bad as I thought.

But it was.

The pitiful little seedling was a pale shadow of its former self, now drowning in a pool of milk. It seemed like it was gasping, "Help me."

I figured my only rational move was to totally hide from Otis for the rest of my natural life. I found myself avoiding the local haunts, grocery shopping way out in Middletown, gassing up in Pennsylvania. It felt like I was on the lam, a marked man, constantly looking over my shoulder.

Otis? Otis was like a woodchuck. He kept popping up everywhere. One morning at the Firehouse Pancake Breakfast he cut me off at the syrup line.

"How's that punkin, Steve?"

How is it that a man who is world famous for growing pumpkins can't even pronounce the word?

"Should be big by now. Pushing fruit?"

"Oh yeah, big," I spoke like a robot. "Pushing fruit. Lots of fruit. All kinds of fruit."

"NO, NO, NO! Just one! You need to remove the rest. You need the energy to go into just one punkin!" He clutched his chest. "Is it on open soil? Needs to be on open soil. No weeds. You have to keep a thirty by thirty square of weed-free open soil."

Thirty by thirty? My entire garden wasn't thirty by thirty.

"And you got to rotate it. Are you rotating it? Every 6 hours. Turn the punkin slightly or it will flatten on one side and split."

Seriously, I could have adopted an actual child and it would have been easier. Otis's face was flush. I saw veins on his neck.

"I'll stop over one day."

I poured coffee instead of syrup on my pancakes.

I returned to the garden just in time to witness the final crushing blow. A cottontail rabbit had breached the fence and was now sitting in a stinky puddle of curdled milk devouring the last pale leaf of the poor sad little pumpkin plant. In a last desperate act, I threw a trowel which completely missed the rabbit but squarely hit (and snapped) the plant off clean.

It was over.

And wouldn't you know it, about then a strange car came bouncing down Laurel Lane. It pulled into our driveway, parked and out stepped Otis

Nolan with his stupid mustache and his stupid baseball cap. Vincent greeted him with a smile and a handshake. From the garden I could see Vincent pointing in my direction. My shoulders slumped with undeniable defeat. The day of reckoning had at last arrived.

I shall spare you the gruesome details but suffice to say that I will not be inducted into the Eternal Order of World Class Giant Pumpkin Growers anytime soon. I will not be playing in the major leagues. I have learned my fate and I have accepted it.

I don't see much of Otis Nolan these days. In fact I heard that he moved down to Georgia. They say he moved to get a longer growing season but I know better. He moved there to get as far away from me as possible. We had our time and I harbor no ill will.

If you happen to bump into Otis, please give him my best.

I've learned a lot since then. And to my credit I have actually succeeded in growing some sizable punkins. Not record breakers, mind you, but big enough to impress gardening neophytes out there.

It's really not that hard to do. You just have to make sure you have the proper pH and a quarter cup of milk twice a day.

8.

We never thought a witch would come to our rescue, but she did.

It started as a brilliant day, sun shining and warm. I was planting snapdragons in the garden. Snapdragons are the best flower. The more you pick the more they bloom. Poke was enjoying my company and the nice weather. But she stepped on a few of the flowers that I had just planted. I waved her off.

"Poke, get out of here."

She circled around and came right back up to me. She didn't understand what I was doing on my hands and knees digging in the dirt. She thought I wanted to play. I was focused on my work and she kept trampling everything.

"Poke, go away!" I scolded and she did.

I finished up and put the shovels and rakes in the shed and as I was closing the shed door I suddenly felt a stabbing pain in the corner of my eye. White hot pain. I flailed my hands at my face and saw something fall to the ground. A wasp. It struggled to right itself.

"You jerk!" I hollered at it. "What did you do that for?! I wasn't bothering you!"

The wasp got up and flew away with a bit of attitude.

"And don't come back!" I shouted after him.

Meanwhile my face was bleating with pain. I felt like I was passing out. I ran cold water from the garden hose over it but already I could feel the swelling. I gathered my wits together and figured I would just go lay down on the hammock. Now where was Poke?

I called her but she didn't come. Probably down the hill sorting out rabbits. My face was throbbing. I flopped down onto the hammock and fell into a dizzy sleep for about an hour. When I woke up Poke was still nowhere to be seen. I could feel my face was puffed up, my eyelids jiggled. I went into the house and looked in a mirror. I looked ridiculous, like a Korean dumpling.

And where was Poke?

Vincent and I both walked around calling for her. He couldn't believe she would just run off. She never had. I couldn't bear to tell him that I had just disciplined her. As the day wore on we really started getting worried.

We knocked on the Dink's door. Ross said he hadn't seen her, which being Ross wasn't saying much. Viola hadn't seen her either. She offered us a slice of acorn buttermilk pie, but neither of us had any appetite. We had to find Poke. She was our child. Ross left us with a comforting thought.

"I hope a coydog didn't git her."

Hoot wasn't home. Stephanie said she hadn't seen Poke either. Hoot was out hunting turkeys. She'd ask him when he got back. Maybe he saw her in the woods. There are a lot of hunters out there. Maybe Poke met up with one. Or maybe with Psycho Pete the taxidermist.

We drove up and down the roads, zigzagging through the hills. A fox darted out across the road but no sign of Poke. Now it was dark. We went home expecting to see her on the porch. But she just wasn't there. It was a sleepless night. At one point thunder and lightning shook the house, followed by driving rain. I couldn't bear the images that haunted me. My poor little girl lost.

Early in the morning, before it was even light, Vincent had to leave on a trip. His last words to me were "please find her."

All that day I hiked the hills and valleys searching for poor Poke. I talked to all kinds of backwoods neighbors. I have to say, even with my swollen Elephant Man face, everyone was very nice and genuinely concerned. I couldn't focus on my artwork and I couldn't bring myself to work on the yard or the garden. I just kept thinking about Poke.

I printed fliers on my computer. I planned to put them on all the telephone poles and trees and at the local shops. Looking at a picture of Poke's sweet little face made me teary. There was a knock at the door. It was Hoot.

"Any luck?"

I just shook my head.

Hoot stepped inside with his big boots. He took off his hat and scratched the top of his head.

"Okay, I've been thinking." You could tell he wanted to help. "I was in those woods all day. I don't want to upset you but there's some bad eggs down there. Some people shouldn't be huntin' is all I'm saying."

It wasn't helpful. I handed him some fliers.

"Yeah, yeah. I'll get these around. I'll give some to Steph. She'll put them at the school. You should talk to the bus drivers. They see everything."

Hoot was heading for the door when he stopped and pawed at his goatee.

"Say, I don't want to get in your business but, did you talk to the witch?"

He studied my fat face for a reaction.

"Sounds crazy I know," he continued, "but that chick finds things. She found Mikey Noeller's dog. And Old Man Grady's horse. That witch, she's got a way with animals, that's for sure. She does that hocus-pocus stuff and they speak to her. She told the Binkwell sisters that their parakeet had flown to Pennsy and sure enough it was captured at a gas station in Wilkes-Barre."

Even my puffiness couldn't hide my look of skepticism.

"Hey," Hoot shrugged, "I'd be the first one to tell you that chick is as crazy as a rooster on a duck farm but what options you got? You want to see your dog again?" He tugged down on his hat and turned to walk away. "Talk to the witch."

I grabbed my jacket and walked down into the woods. It was still and quiet. I yelled out at the top of my lungs, *"POKE!"* But there was nothing. Just silence. The forest had never seemed so empty.

Hoot gave me directions to find the witch's house. Go back to the main road and turn right heading away from town. Turn left on Duncan Hollow Road, six miles, blue mailbox. Boy and I thought we were remote.

It was a long grass driveway to a huge old barn and what looked like an abandoned house except that there were geraniums planted in an old sink on the porch. Everything was painted different pastel colors, even some of the rocks, and no two shutters matched. I parked Rusty at the end of what I thought was still the driveway. I had brought a dozen fresh eggs. When I climbed out of the truck I was immediately greeted by three mewing cats. Two others scurried under the porch and another beneath the barn. It was a sweetly idyllic setting if a bit unplanned. There were flowers everywhere and unseen wind chimes tinkling in the gentle breeze. Kind of weird, but I really couldn't tell where the front door was.

"Hello...?" I called out.

I thought I heard something so I walked around toward the barn and came face to face with a huge black bear. You know the expression "pooped in my pants"? Well the only reason I didn't was because I didn't have time. I screamed out like a cheerleader and threw the carton of eggs at the bear. The bear huffed snot. I stumbled backwards shouting "NO! NO!" I dove into my truck and slammed the door.

Fortunately the bear was distracted by the broken eggs. It lapped them off the grass with its giant tongue, shells and all. I fumbled for my keys. Then out of nowhere a slender blonde woman appeared holding a bouquet of thistle. I beeped the horn and waved my arm to warn her but she didn't seem troubled at all. In fact she walked right up to the bear and placed her hand on its shoulder. She leaned down and whispered in the bear's ear then pointed to the forest. With a few final licks and an indignant grunt the bear quietly lumbered off toward the woods. The woman approached my truck.

She was somehow ageless. Perhaps in her fifties, give or take ten years, with soft pale features and a single braid of blonde (or was it grey?) hair. She wore a long cotton skirt and her feet were bare. I rolled down the window just a crack, still breathing like I had run a marathon.

"I'm so sorry about that," she cooed. "That's just Pansy. I think you frightened her."

"Me? *Her!?*"

My hands were shaking as I retrieved a flyer and slipped it to the woman through the space in the window.

"I'm looking for my dog."

She looked at the picture of Poke, pressed it to her breast, closed her eyes and moaned.

"Sweet child."

The bear was nowhere in sight but it still took some convincing to get me out of the truck and into her house. The woman's name was Helen Solowsky but she preferred to go by her Wicca name which was Trillium. It occurred to me that her house was surprisingly cheerful, for someone who practiced witchcraft. I didn't see any black cats, but I sure saw every other color. On every chair and every table, including the one we were sitting at in the kitchen. Trillium poured me a cup of hot tea. She said it was a blend of herbs that would relieve the swelling in my face. It smelled like mint and jasmine and skunk. And it tasted like that too.

"I haven't seen her for forty-eight hours now," I sighed. "I'm really worried. She's my baby."

Trillium tilted the tea pot on its side and spilled some of the wet tea leaves onto a chipped china plate. She pushed a cat aside and rocked the plate in circles, studying the swill of tea. She spoke without looking up.

"She's alive."

It's strange to say, but when your heart is hurting like mine... I just believed her somehow.

"I feel kind of bad," I said and looked down at my teacup. "I scolded her."

Trillium kept swirling and reading the tea.

"You were short with her," she said insightfully. "She understands. She wants you to know that she forgives you."

I started squirming a bit. Wait a second, is this woman a nut job?

Suddenly she stopped rocking the dish. She squinted her eyes and scrutinized the tea leaves.

"I see a green door."

I spit a mouthful of tea back into the cup. Who was I kidding, this stuff tasted awful and this lady was a loon. I tried to think of a polite way to say *adios senorita,* but suddenly Trillium stared up at me with a revelation.

"Your father knows where she is."

Okay that was enough. I scooted my chair back and stood up.

We Hillfolk

"Well I really have to get going," I said as I nudged several cats out of the way. "I have to keep looking for her while it's light out." I felt for my wallet. "Do I owe you any money... for...?"

I motioned toward the plate of tea leaves. Trillium smiled at me.

"Don't be silly. You brought eggs for Pansy."

Oh, that's right, that stupid bear. How was I going to get out of here without being mauled? I tripped over a cat on my way to the door. I paused and stared out the kitchen window looking to see that the coast was clear. Trillium quietly walked up beside me. She gently placed her hand on mine and looked deep into my eyes.

"Talk to your father. He knows where she is."

I put up every last flier. Even on trees and telephone poles that I knew no one would ever see. It was difficult driving down Laurel Lane returning to a Poke-less house. I tossed my keys on the kitchen counter. Curiously, the swelling in my face had gone away.

I went out and sat on the little bench in the garden, alone, silent and very depressed. The sun was setting over the valley, another day ending without my dog. Such a void. Was she out there somewhere, lost in that vast wilderness? My eyes welled up with tears. It's hard to lose a dog, especially a good one. Vincent was going to be heartbroken. I gazed out over the far horizon and sighed. Then I said out loud, "Dad... where is Poke?"

And that's when I heard a *thump - bump!*

It came from the garden shed. I wasn't sure what it was. I walked over to the shed. It couldn't be... I opened the green door and there she was!

We rolled on the ground and hugged and kissed, her tail was wagging non-stop.

The wasp sting had blinded me with pain, and I unknowingly locked poor Poke in the tool shed for almost three days. She thought she was being punished because I had scolded her so like a good girl she just stayed quiet. I had even yelled "jerk!" at that wasp, maybe Poke thought I was yelling at her. I felt horrible for what I had so stupidly done but overjoyed to have my little Pokie back again.

She was very thirsty. I gave her a drink from the garden hose and I made her a big bowl of food and she ate it all. The way she was prancing around and biting at my cuffs I could tell she really did forgive me and just wanted to play.

9.

Vincent went out to buy chicken feed and came home with a geriatric patient.

Someone had left a cardboard box on the doorstep of the feed mill and inside was a very elderly chicken. The old girl was well past her egg laying years and there wasn't enough meat on her scrawny bones to make a sandwich. As chickens go, she was a lame duck. She was pretty much worthless, everyone agreed. Everyone, that is, except Vincent.

Vincent saw something of value in that paltry poultry, something others may have overlooked, something more valuable than meat or eggs. He saw a friend. He named her B.B. because she was black and blind. Her eyes were milky with cataracts and she could barely hobble on her spindly chicken legs and yet her attitude was positive.

Every morning Vincent opened the henhouse, filled the feeders, collected the eggs and tended to the flock. Too nearsighted and arthritic to fly down from the perch on her own, B.B. would wait patiently for Vincent's helping hands. She would cluck hello as he lovingly picked her up, carried her outside and set her down on a grassy knoll in the filtered shade of a barberry scrub.

Vincent found that blind B.B. could only eat her food if she could figure out where it was. He searched the forest and found the perfect slab of Catskill bluestone to serve as her banquet table. Each day he made sure that B.B. had a bowl of fresh water and a handful of scratch grain spread out on the bluestone. Sometimes he would even cook some pasta or rice for her. B.B. would always chortle a thank you.

B.B. never let her physical limitations dampen her bright outlook. She enjoyed her quiet days in the cool shade, squinting and pecking at her private buffet. The rest of the flock instinctively knew to give the old dowager her space.

One morning, Vincent was heading out to the tool shed when he was suddenly horrified to see a huge red-tailed hawk standing squarely with its talons clenched on poor B.B.'s lifeless body.

Vincent waved his arms and screamed out.

"NO HAWK! SCRAM!"

He ran at the raptor and it flew up and away leaving B.B.'s dead body slumped on the bluestone, beak open and tongue out. It was a sad sight indeed.

Vincent kneeled down and brushed away some plucked feathers.

"Aw, sorry B.B.," he sighed. "You were a good old girl."

Vincent resolved himself to B.B.'s fate. She had a good long run, for a chicken. Such is the circle of life on the farmstead.

Vincent decided it would be most fitting to bury her right there at her favorite spot in the filtered shade of the barberry scrub. Solemnly he headed back down the hill to retrieve a spade from the tool shed.

Shovel in hand, Vincent headed back and was completely overjoyed to discover a slightly dazed but as always cheerful B.B. sitting up straight, squinting in the sunlight, contently pecking at the confetti of grain on her bluestone table. She had defied death.

"B.B. you're okay!" Vincent marveled at the little hen's resilience. "You're going to get an extra handful of scratch today and maybe later some pasta."

Vincent strolled back down to the shed, happy to be putting the shovel away. He scooped a handful of scratch, walked back up the knoll and--- *son of a bitch!*

That big red-tailed hawk was back once again, with its talons clenched on B.B.'s crumpled body. Vincent threw the grain at it.

"NO HAWK! GET AWAY!"

Once again the hawk flew off.

Only this time the hawk clutched tightly, taking B.B. with him.

With an agonizing groan, Vincent could do nothing more than watch as B.B. was carried away in the grip of the hawk just like Dorothy was by the flying monkeys.

They disappeared over the mountain never to be seen again.

We now use B.B.'s bluestone as our front step.

10.

Flower competition is not a pretty business.

The whole thing started on a whim. I read in the local paper that the Big Bloomers Garden Club would once again be sponsoring this year's flower competition at the Country Fair.

"Wouldn't it be fun to win a blue ribbon?" I said to Vincent.

We had some nice dahlias growing in the garden. I really didn't do anything special to get them so nice; they just were. I bought the tubers at the feed store and stuck them in the ground and they grew by themselves. Maybe I watered them once or twice, and maybe I threw a little bone meal on them when I happened to find some in a bag in the tool shed, but really I didn't do much of anything else. That said, they looked pretty amazing. Definite show quality.

This blue ribbon wasn't just some dollar store trinket from a big plastic bag full of blue ribbons. The Big Bloomers had to special order it. It was hand crafted in Bangladesh and probably cost, oh, I'm guessing in the neighborhood of at least twenty five bucks. Maybe more. It was a bold state fair blue and splendidly embossed with large gold letters that proclaimed BEST OF SHOW. They only give out one. And therein lies the problem.

I had to have it.

The by-laws clearly state that competitors can only enter one specimen in the Best of Show division. To choose just one, was going to be a bit of a challenge, especially for me. I have no problem making life changing decisions in a snap. Quit my job, move from California, buy a house in the Catskills. Snap! Snap! Snap! But make a little decision like what color shirt to wear...

I could wear the blue shirt, but does it make me look pale? The yellow is nice. Or would it be too bright? I could always wear the white one. But what if I get there and everybody is wearing black?

Choose my best dahlia for a shot at a blue ribbon? Not easy.

One of the dahlias in our garden was a variety known as Kiss-Me-Kate, and it was huge. Some of these dahlia blossoms can get to be twelve inches across and this one was close to that, I swear. Only problem, Kiss-Me-Kate was white.

Would a white flower be dynamic enough to impress a judge? Or should I go with something more vibrant like the orange and red dahlia, Tequila Sunrise? Of course the soft subtle hues of Baby Jane might work, were I to choose a more understated approach. But then who could argue with the classic balance of color and form in the dahlia so aptly named Madame Vanderbilt? Or was that too obvious a choice? Should I push the envelope and enter Mr. Bojangles?

Decisions. Decisions.

I got Vincent out to the garden for his opinion. He took a quick look around.

"That one."

"You're serious?" I was flabbergasted. "Monty's Surprise?"

"That one," he repeated as he walked away.

You have to admire that man's decisiveness.

The fairgrounds are just across a covered bridge on an open hillside. It's a sprawling collection of red barns, livestock paddocks, ticket booths and a small amphitheater, all of which for most of the year sits empty and closed up like a ghost town. But for one weekend each August the place comes alive with throngs of fairgoers who travel from as far away as Connecticut or even Pennsylvania to stroll about the grounds, enjoying the festivities while feasting on pulled pork and German brats.

This steamy summer weekend is always jam-packed with a full schedule of draw horse competitions and pie bake-offs. Qualified judges meander from stall to stall carefully evaluating the lovingly groomed standards of cows, goats, swine, poultry and rabbits. At night the midway becomes a kaleidoscope of whirling rides and games of chance.

Drop off for the flower competition was between 7:00 and 8:00 Friday morning. According to the by-laws no flower would be accepted one minute earlier or one minute later. And you have to provide your own vase. I decided to go with a Mason jar, you know, to keep with that country fair theme. Once through the front gate, I stepped in to a nearby port-a-john and refilled the jar with fresh water.

The flowers were all displayed in a small red barn directly across from Freda's Funnel Cakes. Just to play it cool, I got there at about 7:15. The place was already crowded with the other flower exhibitors. You have never seen so many white perms in one room. It looked like a snowball fight. A clique of a dozen or so ladies and a little Chinese guy had gathered around the display benches each vying for prime vase location.

I stepped up with Monty's Surprise and immediately I could feel everyone eyeing me suspiciously. New meat on the chopping block. Just who does he think he is? I smiled, but I felt about as welcome as an April blizzard.

The first thing you have to do is go over to the judges table and fill out a couple of forms. It's all very official. They give you a card with your name on it and then you place your vase in the exhibit area. I scanned the shelves. The other flowers were chumps compared to mine. I muscled in on some prime real estate on the third tier, right between a tea rose and a marigold. Seriously, a marigold. Don't make me laugh. You could stop at the gas station on your way to the fair and pick a marigold out of a planter box.

Monty's Surprise looked proud and handsome. The other flowers didn't even come close. Just a few feet away I noticed a stately delphinium that could have been a bit of a threat, but it was almost too tall and it was crooked in its vase so I was still feeling pretty confident.

Then at five minutes to eight an extremely tall woman with a crane's beak for a nose strutted up to the officials table carrying...yes, a dahlia. And wouldn't you know it, Kiss-Me-Kate. Not as big or robust as the one back at home in our garden but definitely a contender and the officials at the table all ooohed and ahhhed. The worst part was that she brought it in some fancy shmancy vase. I think it was crystal!

I didn't know we could do that. I thought this was a country fair. Vases don't count, do they?

It was down to the wire so they hurried to find a place for her dahlia. Unfortunately, since the shelves were crowded, someone shoved mine to one side and squeezed her Kiss-Me-Kate in between my dahlia and the marigold.

Monty looked small next to Kate.

At 8:00 sharp one of the officials rang a little bell and that was that. No more entries would be accepted and no more touching or arranging flowers. The next hour was dedicated to public viewing. Everyone was sort of milling around quietly, lots of hushed whispers and discreet pointing.

The crane beaked lady joined the white haired ladies and the little Chinese guy. They were talking about me. I could tell. You can always tell.

At one point the crane lady strutted by. She looked down her beak at me.

"Monty's Surprise?" she said.

"Kiss-Me-Kate?" I replied.

The gloves were off.

Vincent walked in chomping on a churro. He nudged me and asked me how it was going. I shrugged and told him that I was having second thoughts about our decision to go with Monty's Surprise. And that maybe we should have played it safe and chosen Madame Vanderbilt or even Mr. Bojangles. Vincent assured me I was over-thinking things, as usual, but then his eyes lit up.

"Wow look at that white one."

"Yes, I see the white one," I muttered. "Kiss-Me-Kate. We have one. Back home in the garden. You told me not to pick it."

"I did?" Vincent frowned.

"Plus, it's in a crystal vase. Crystal. Mine is in a jar, Vincent. A jar." I glared at him. "A jar with a chip in it."

"Oh, don't worry," Vincent tried to calm me. "You'll get second place for sure."

"I don't want second place," I said through a clenched grin. "I didn't come here for second place. There are fourteen second places."

I heard heavy boots on the wood plank floor and in walked Hoot and Stephanie.

"So, did you get your blue ribbon?" Hoot bellowed.

Did he have to be so loud?

"Viola Dink just got a blue ribbon for her venison beet pie," he added.

Having once sampled a slice of Viola's venison beet pie, I can assure you that it is every bit as scrumptious as you'd imagine.

Hoot looked over at the flower display.

"That white one yours?" he asked. "You'll win for sure."

Vincent chuckled.

"Anyway," Hoot said. "Just came to wish you good luck. We got to head over to the animal husbandry barn. I'm judging the goats."

"Oh, we want to get goats," Vincent said.

"No, we don't," I intercepted.

"Do they have the little pygmies?" Vincent asked. "I'll go with you. I have to see them."

"What do you know about judging goats, Hoot?" I asked.

"I know enough not to bend over and tie my shoe in a goat pen."

Stephanie rolled her eyes.

"Last year he judged the zucchinis."

Hoot stuck out his chin.

"That was some stiff competition there."

No sooner had they left when Neil came lumbering in wolfing down a pink beehive of cotton candy.

"That is so gross," I said. "How can you buy that stuff?"

"I didn't buy it," he said. "I found it." Then he looked over at the flowers. "So did you win anything?"

"The judging is in an hour."

"Whoa... check out that white one. That yours?"

"No," I sighed. "Mine is the one next to it."

"That dinky one?"

"Not the marigold. The one to the left."

"Oh, too bad," Neil said. "Too bad it's not the white one."

He took a chomp of his cotton candy.

"Is that real?" he continued. "That white one? That is the most beautiful flower I have ever seen."

"Don't you have some dumpster diving to do?"

Neil nudged me, leaned in close and whispered.

"You want me to pee on it?"

"What?"

"That white flower," Neil said. "I could sneak it around back and pee on it. Make it wilt."

"I'm sure it would." I shook my head. "I think that cotton candy is affecting your brain."

"You want some?"

"No. But thank you."

I stepped away from him, but he followed me.

"What about battery acid?" Neil whispered. He made a little pistol motion with his hand. "I could spritz it with battery acid."

"I really think you need counseling."

"Suit yourself." Neil leaned in close and scrutinized the flowers. "I hate to inform you, my friend, but I think <u>you</u> got spritzed."

"What are you talking about?"

I leaned in to have a closer look. Sure enough, Neil was right. Monty's Surprise was looking gaunt and wilted.

What was happening? Could it be? Was someone here actually capable of flower sabotage?

I glanced over at the white-haired clique. They all avoided eye contact with me, especially the Chinese guy.

Neil took several whiffs with his big nostrils.

"I smell bleach."

I know you are thinking that a flower competition could never be this ruthless. But floriculture has a well documented history of vicious coldblooded rivalries. In the early 1900's, orchid collectors searching the world's jungles not only faced a constant threat of disease, starvation and hostile natives, but also terrible acts from rival collectors that included thievery, sabotage and even murder. I could only hope it wouldn't come to that.

I very gently caressed Monty's petals. They were flaccid and limp. The crane glared at me.

"No more arranging the flowers!" she squawked, which, of course, directed the attention of the entire room onto me. I held up my palms.

"I was just..."

I tried to say something. Then one of the officials barked at Neil.

"There is no food or beverages allowed in here!"

"I was just leaving," he announced then fake punched me and said, "Knock 'em dead." Neil headed out the door in search of more junk food.

One of the officials rang the little bell to announce that the judging was about to begin. Everyone politely applauded as an official introduced each judge (two women and one man) and stated their various qualifications. I was a tad taken back when the crane leaned in and gave the man judge a little peck on the cheek.

Wait a second... is that allowed?

The three distinguished judges quietly made their way over to the display shelves, pencils and clipboards in hand. A hush came over the room. There was a tension in the air that you could cut with floral scissors. This was shaping up to be a real nail biter.

I got a lump in my throat when I saw the judges quietly swoon when they got to the crane's Kiss-Me-Kate dahlia. They all nodded and jotted down notes on their clipboards.

When they got to my Monty's Surprise it seemed as if they just sort of glossed right over it. I don't think the man judge even paused at all. Then horror of horrors! Right before everyone's eyes a petal fell from Monty onto the shelf.

Everyone froze. The Chinese guy gasped.

The judges looked at Monty's Surprise and then at each other. They jotted notes on their clipboards and moved on.

But I wasn't having it. You can only push me so far. I pointed my finger in the air.

"Somebody sabotaged my flower!"

Everyone gasped.

I marched up to the display shelves and grabbed the Mason jar, spilling some of the water.

"Smell it. Smell this water. It smells like bleach!"

A murmur rumbled through the crowd like a thunder storm at a garden party. I stood defiant but no one fessed up. We were going to get to the bottom of this. We could do it the easy way or we could do it the hard way, but a cheater was going to get nipped in the bud. Then the crane lady spoke up.

"Where did you get that water from?"

"The port-o-john," I said.

Everyone chuckled. From her lofty height the crane smiled.

"They chlorinate that water."

The Chinese guy snickered.

They'd be talking about this one at garden club meetings for years to come.

Monty's Surprise got an honorable mention.

113

It came out of a big plastic bag full of yellow ribbons. The crane got a second place for her Kiss-Me-Kate. (Fixed.)

And Best of Show? The blue ribbon went to the marigold. Seriously. The marigold.

I am done with flower competitions. I just don't have the stomach for it.

Next year, I decided, I'm going to enter a goat.

11.

The morning sparkled.

I was in my art shed working on an assignment. I had been commissioned to do some creepy children's drawings for a Robert DeNiro movie. The director wanted an illustrator who could think like a child but was a little bit twisted. Somehow my name came up, and I got the gig. It would be a good infusion of money.

Vincent and Poke had driven Rusty down into the woods to gather some firewood. With Hoot's guidance, Vincent had become quite skilled at using a chainsaw. I could hear it whirring in the distance.

It was one of those days when everything was just working. Sunny, warm, living in the country and making money. It couldn't be better. I heard the truck and looked out the studio window to see Vincent driving into the backyard with a full load of logs, Poke trotting along side. I went out to meet them.

"That's a lot of wood!" I said.

Vincent opened the truck door and climbed out. He lifted the chainsaw out of the back of the truck and without saying a word he walked me around to the passenger side to show me a smashed side mirror, dangling against the door by a cable. The poor little truck was rusting away and now this.

"What happened?" I asked.

Vincent shrugged.

"I kind of hit a tree."

It wasn't completely registering. I figured I'd help him unload, and I'd get a logical explanation. When I went to take the chainsaw from him I could smell alcohol. No further explanation was necessary.

I could no longer deny that Vincent was drinking too much. Several times I had gone to pour myself a glass of wine and was surprised to find the bottle empty when I was sure it was full just the day before. You hear stories about people who abuse alcohol hiding bottles around the house. But I was finding the opposite true. I found myself hiding bottles from Vincent so that when I wanted a glass of wine it would be there. If I didn't hide it, it would be gone. A dark reality settled in. I confronted Vincent.

"You were drinking and operating a chainsaw?"

"No," he said but it sounded weak. "Don't make a big deal out of this, Scott."

When a person says your name it can take the conversation to a disturbing new level.

"Really," I said, flipping the broken mirror against the dented door. "It's not a big deal. Could we get someone else's opinion? What would my brothers say? What would your family say? What if we ask Hoot what he thinks about drinking and chain sawing?"

"Stop it."

"No Vincent. You stop it," I said and I walked off.

It was a terrible moment in my life. I felt like I had been punched in the stomach. I didn't know what to do. My dad always said when something is troubling you, go into nature. Nature soothes the soul.

I headed down Laurel Lane, past Louise's trailer and up into the woods. Poke tore a crisscross pattern through the woods ahead of me.

At some point I came upon a long forgotten trail, two grassy tire ruts that snaked through the forest and up into the hills. From the treetops, a lone raven announced my presence.

How was it that a day could so quickly turn from happiness to shit?

In time, I lost sight of Poke. I called to her once, but I was alone. I rounded a corner and was quite surprised to come upon an abandoned house. It was just the empty shell of a little farmhouse with broken windows and a tree growing up through a hole in the roof.

I cautiously stepped up onto the porch. The floorboards groaned underfoot with threats of cracking. The old house was listing to one side, forcing the front door ajar. I entered a little parlor. The dated wallpaper was streaked and stained from years of a leaking roof.

To the left there was a kitchen. Missing cupboard doors revealed empty shelves, and against one wall was an old farm sink and woodstove. A teacup on the counter looked as if someone had just placed it there moments ago, except that it was upholstered with a thick layer of grey dust.

I could feel a ghostly presence, the echoes of humans gone, of past lives.

Who left that teacup? Who left that dishtowel hanging on a hook?

Slowly, I climbed the creaky staircase to the second floor landing and came upon three tiny bedrooms. A bird had built its nest on a light fixture that hung from the ceiling in the middle of one room. Startled by my intrusion it flew out through a broken window to a nearby tree branch and scolded me with angry chirps.

I gazed out the window at the enormous Neversink Reservoir. The surrounding pristine wilderness keeps this water supply pure for the city.

On the forest floor below Poke hurried by, her tail in the air, her nose to the ground and squirrels on her mind.

The room was completely void of furniture except for an old wooden hutch. Its veneer cracked and splitting, its drawers warped and swollen by time. They were empty except for a mouse nest of chewed paper and a scattering of turds. The top drawer was stuck, but I forced it opened. It too was empty except for a small but very classic perfume bottle. The perfume had long ago evaporated, and now all that remained was a thin crescent of yellowed resin. I tried to squeeze the little spritzer, but it was brittle and fell apart. The cap was tarnished blue green and encrusted with mineral deposit.

Somehow the little bottle had a charm to it. I'm sure it held a story.

I put it to my nose and looked out across the reservoir. I could barely detect the last faint scent of sweet perfume.

Anna woke to the sharp ping of a pebble hitting the glass of her window. She climbed out of bed and quickly wrapped herself in a cotton robe. Another ping. Anna hurried to the window. She opened it and looked down to see Mary Bender's older brother Henry. Anna whisper-shouted down to him.

"Henry Bender, what are you doing here?! If you wake Mamma and Pa, we will both get a switch."

"Don't forget your promise," Henry whispered back.

The young people of the town of Neversink had played a game of baseball against the young people of the town of Bittersweet. Henry told Anna that if he got a home run she would have to kiss him. Indeed he did hit the winning home run for Neversink, and now he had come to collect.

"I never agreed. You just said it like a president," she hushed. "You are trouble, Henry Bender. Now go away before my pa shoots rock salt at you."

The next Sunday at church Henry Bender sat directly behind Anna. He kept bumping the back of Anna's pew. At one point Henry whispered in the smallest voice ever.

"Don't forget your promise."

Anna's pa turned around and gave him such a stare.

Afterwards Pastor Higgins commented, "Why Henry Bender, what brings you to church today?"

Henry walked past Anna's house every day after school, even though the school was on the other side of the valley and not on the road to his house at all.

When summer came, Anna's pa hired Henry to help with the cows.

"If that boy's going to be coming around here all the time, he might as well do some work."

At last one summer day, between the milk parlor and the meadow Anna kept her promise. Even though she never said she would.

"You are trouble, Henry Bender," she whispered.

But then a shadow filled the valley, and what once was would never be again.

Some very serious men who wore dark ties and shiny shoes came and told the people that they would have to leave. Other people, people who lived in the city far away needed their valley. A great dam was to be built and soon the valley would become a lake, a reservoir of water.

The towns of Neversink and Bittersweet, the farms, the homes, the pastures, the school and even the church would disappear forever. The men with the shiny shoes told the people of the valley that they would be relocated and compensated. It was a good thing for everyone, they said. Anna's pa did not agree. His father had farmed this valley and his father's father too. But big machines had already begun to move the hillside.

Then one autumn day, between the milk parlor and the meadow, Henry Bender told Anna that he and all the boys of the valley were being called to serve in the military. Anna begged Henry not to go. They could run away together. Nothing mattered anymore. Henry said he had to go but he promised he'd come back. Anna sobbed.

"What if you see other places and don't want to come back? What if you come back and nothing is here anymore?"

Henry handed Anna a small brown bag tied with twine. Anna opened it to find a bottle of perfume with a shiny silver cap. She squeezed a mist just below her neck. It was the sweetest scent she had ever known. Henry kissed Anna's neck and captured her sweetness.

"What if you get hurt?" Anna wiped away her tears. "What if..."

Henry brushed back her hair.

"Write to me every day. And spray each letter with your perfume. It will get me through whatever I have to face."

"But they are moving our house up into the mountain," Anna cried. "How will you find me again?"

Henry smiled and held Anna in his arms.

"I will find you," he said. "I promise."

I heard a dog barking and I looked out the window. It was Poke tromping down the hillside. Then I heard a voice calling out. A shadowy figure made its way into a clearing. It was Vincent.

"Hello. I'm up here," I called out. Vincent looked up at me in the second story window.

"I followed Poke," Vincent said. "She led me right to you."

I made my way back down the rickety staircase and met up with Vincent in the kitchen.

"Wow, this is a cool old place," he said. "I wonder who lived here."

"If walls could talk."

I showed Vincent the perfume bottle. He said I should do a painting of it. Then he looked at me.

"I think maybe I need help."

I nodded. "I think maybe we do."

The sun was setting over the reservoir as we made our way back home.

12.

City dwellers have got it made.

They just go to the end of the hall, open a magic door and toss their garbage in. The garbage falls down into a vast cavern where gnomes collect it and cart it off. We country bumpkins, on the other hand, are forced to deal with the waste we create. There is no garbage pick-up. You are the garbage man.

Of course recycling plays a huge part. The goal is to compartmentalize everything, a giant puzzle of stacked newspapers and rinsed bean cans. This goes here, that goes there. My system is quite impressive. Then there's my compost pile, an amassment of all things vegetable. A true work of art.

But it's the rest of the garbage that can be a challenge, the things that don't fit in any recycle category. Things like moldy hummus and half eaten tuna sandwiches. This category of garbage is a ticking time bomb that constantly forces your hand and makes trips to the dump a weekly sacrament.

You can get away with stockpiling garbage along the far side of your garage for only so long before it becomes an aromatic invitation that cordially invites flies, dogs, raccoons and black bears to a free banquet. There is nothing more annoying than to wake up in the morning and discover your garbage cans overturned and all your private, smelly rubbish spread out across the driveway like a Rorschach test.

Catskill winters can ease your dump run frequency a bit. Animals are for the most part hibernating and the snow and cold keeps everything sufficiently refrigerated. Sometimes our winter garbage piles up so much that the end of the driveway looks like a plane crash in the Andes.

For some reason the word "dump" is not politically correct these days. It is frowned upon to refer to the place where we throw our old couches and fish bones as a dump. Instead it is given one of any number of lofty titles such as "Recycle Center", "Collection Facility", "Refuse Yard" or as in our case, "Transfer Station."

To me, the term "transfer station" conjures up images of smartly dressed gentleman and ladies with parasols boarding steam trains bound for Paris or Marrakesh. But trust me; you can't get to Paris from this dump. Sorry, *Transfer Station*.

Our transfer station is a gated community. It's a vast, fenced-in expanse of sun blessed acreage that would probably have been some very prime real estate were it not for the fact that years ago our forefathers unanimously agreed that this was the best place to throw all our crap.

The comings and goings at our transfer station are carefully managed by three notable gentlemen: Manny the Mulcher , Handsome Hank, and Paul.

He's called Manny the Mulcher because just inside the gate is his proud conception, a huge pile of mulch. It was created from years of people dumping yard debris, leaves and branches in one mountainous pile. Manny uses the big backhoe dozer to move it around, stir it and otherwise sculpt it. He takes great pride in his mulch pile.

Handsome Hank is by no means handsome when viewed in regular society. But for a guy who works at a dump, he's a real looker.

And Paul is just Paul.

These three gents make sure everyone abides by the many unspoken yet tightly monitored rituals one must address when entering the gates of the Transfer Station. You will very quickly realize that you are not going to just pull up and start chucking stuff into the nearest dumpster. Everything is very well orchestrated. There are rules that must be followed in this facility. And Manny the Mulcher is Grand Poobah.

But I'm getting ahead of myself.

You won't even get past the front gates of the Transfer Station until you first stop in and see Donna or Peggy at the town hall and buy a yearly pass. It's like an exclusive club. The Transfer Station Club. You've got to pay your dues but you get a little sticker that says *you belong*. Every year it's a different color. A bit of a status comes with seeing how many years worth of stickers you can collect on your sun visor.

But it doesn't stop there. In addition to that pass, you have to buy a pack of punch cards in order to dump anything that isn't recyclable. It's like a club within a club.

Metal cans go into one dumpster, glass bottles in another. For some reason plastic bottles can go together with metal cans but _never_ plastic or metal with glass. It can be a tricky recipe to juggle, like Rock, Scissors, Paper.

All big metal objects (that's toaster oven and larger) get dropped down into the main dumpster. This includes your bedsprings, TV antennas, old tire rims, and all home furnishings from the 1970's.

It is very important that you look down into the dumpster before you toss anything in.

Two reasons:

1.) You never know, there might be something very cool down there that some fool didn't realize was a valued treasure. Once an item is in the dumpster it's fair game. If you can reach it, you can have it. Free! One time I found a steel go-cart frame (and it was hardly even bent that much) and another time I found an emu feeder. I'm serious, to feed emu! I had a bit of trouble getting it to dispense the feed and unfortunately we don't have an emu.

And 2.) If you happen to spot an old style television set or window frames with the glass still intact you want to properly aim your tire rim toss to get the biggest smash.

Every time I drive into the Transfer Station I get a slight case of the butterflies. Everyone seems to know exactly what goes where and why. I am always just a little on edge, never 100% confident about proper Transfer Station protocol.

Can I just toss the entire plastic bag full of plastic bottles into the dumpster or do I have to first open the bag and empty the bottles out and then the bag goes somewhere else? Will an alarm go off if I throw a bundle of magazines in the dumpster labeled CARDBOARD ONLY?

More often than not I arrive with an entire truckload of trash. That's when I get really nervous because they make you back the truck up to the edge of a concrete abutment that overlooks a lower level container. I have visual myopia and it makes backing up extremely challenging for me, even at the supermarket. But there is no telling that to Manny, his gloved hand waving me back.

"C'mon...C'mon...C'mon...C'mon..., WHOA!"

It's nerve racking enough to be watching that waving glove in the rearview mirror; you also have to navigate between two steel posts as your truck creeps toward a ten foot drop-off into an abyss of garbage. Drivers have gone over. We've all heard the stories. Everyone watches, cell phone cameras at the ready.

Once I am finally properly docked in the slip and Manny gives the gloved thumbs up, I breathe a sigh of relief. The Eagle has landed. I always feel so accomplished. There is something very manly about being able to successfully back up a truck. And I always bring a pair of rubber gloves to protect my delicate hands.

Manny will sort of help you unload but he's mostly on the prowl for copper. At a dump, copper is gold. It can be sold by the pound for cash across the county at the mother dump. Manny snags any and all pieces of copper pipe, roof flashing and even old cookware. Rumor has it he's had some impressive payouts. It's how he and Luella financed their 52" television.

Manny's not much of a talker. He's more of a grunter. Two short grunts mean no and one grunt with a raised inflection at the end means yes. On the rare occasion that he does converse, it's in short mumbled sentences that are very difficult to understand. He just doesn't enunciate. You get the feeling that as a baby he learned to speak from imitating the family coonhound.

One time he said to me, "Jur jruk asgot a flateer." I thought he was speaking Swedish. It was like playing the Sgt. Pepper album backwards. It wasn't until I got halfway home and I suddenly heard this horrible thumping sound that I realized he had actually said, "Your truck has got a flat tire."

Driving away from the Transfer Station with an empty truck one experiences an exhilarating feeling of nirvana. The great weight of your carbon footprint is off your shoulders. That said, I have to admit I was born with the gene that makes me virtually incapable of leaving any garbage facility without taking a keepsake home with me.

One time I peered over the edge and down into a mostly empty container and was amazed to see a perfectly good antique stove resting on its back at the bottom. It was like finding the lost ark. How could someone just throw this piece of history into a dumpster? I am talking about an authentic cast iron, wood fired cook stove with white enameled legs and those flat iron circles that fit on the top.

I looked around to make sure the coast was clear. True, anything is free grabs but this was going to require actually jumping down into the container and humping the stove up. Manny was off stirring his mulch pile, Handsome Hank was flirting with some ladies at the NEWSPAPER ONLY bin and Paul was just Paul.

I seized the moment and hopped down onto the stove like a lemur on a beetle. It was a lot bigger than I thought and heavy as hell. Fortunately the different sections were very easy to disassemble. I hoisted each piece up over my head and onto the pavement above. I would just have to remember how it all went back together.

I then pulled myself up and shimmied back out of the dumpster, an athletic effort that is each year becoming more of a challenge. As I was loading the various sections into the back of my truck Manny came strolling up. He took one look at what I was doing and grinned from ear to ear.

"Jul be sur ja tok dis pisha jit om."

I wasn't exactly sure what he said, but obviously he was envious of my find.

Once I got the stove home, I spread the pieces out on the front lawn and went to work with a hose, a scrub brush and a bucket of hot soapy water. I spent the rest of that afternoon scrubbing that vintage treasure, that historic art piece. It stunk of mice.

I will admit that it was a bit of a conundrum getting it all reassembled properly. Somehow I ended up with six extra pieces. And the oven door didn't quite line up right.

Is this thing even going to work or will it catch the house on fire? Is it going to leak carbon monoxide? Why does it still smell like mice?

At this point I thought to measure it and realized that it would not fit through any door of our house. The front porch was probably not the most convenient location for a woodstove.

It was in that moment of clarity that my brain was able to decipher exactly what Manny had said.

"You'll be sorry you took this piece of shit home."

The next morning, Handsome Hank and Paul helped me heave the woodstove off the bed of my truck and back into the big dumpster. I had basically hauled a huge piece of junk home, scrubbed and washed it and then hauled it back again. It crashed square on a big old television set that exploded with a mighty smash.

Even Manny was impressed.

"Dash o gudon!"

13.

We woke one morning to a changed world.

It didn't immediately appear any different. The sun came up, the birds were singing, Poke was out herding chipmunks, but now... we could get married. With the flick of some bureaucratic switch, New York State bestowed upon us the right to legally be what we already were.

Yet, in some way Vincent suddenly looked different to me, as I'm sure that I looked different to him. We didn't say anything, just shared passing glances as we went about our morning rituals, a quiet taking of inventory.

Now what do we do?

For the last ten years we had lulled ourselves into a comfortable arrangement of together forever, for now. Marriage was something other people did. Suddenly a new day had dawned and we could seal the deal with forty five bucks and an embossed stamp from Peggy the town clerk.

I can see her now, smiling at us through her Chiclet teeth. "Good luck, you guys," she would say with genuine sentiment and to which I would reply, "Thanks, Peggy. Oh, and while you're at it. We also need a punch card for the Transfer Station. Can I write one check for both?" (You can.)

I didn't choose to be the way I am. I chose to be much taller with a thick head of hair. But for whatever reason, things didn't turn out the way I had planned.

I swaggered through grade school with a cocky smile, the smile of a boy who knew he would one day marry a beautiful blonde actress and together they would raise their six perfect children on a one-hundred-acre bunny farm. By about fifth grade, just as puberty set in so did a sobering reality. The road to the bunny farm was about to deviate.

It hit young me like a punch in the gut. The farm, the beautiful wife and the six perfect children all vaporized. I was left with a great emptiness, alone to battle my terrible, shameful curse and watch as my little classmates peddled happily ahead toward my American Dream. All alone, I fought my splintered reality.

Not that. Not me. Someone else. Just not me.

It was a long, dark Mordor tunnel in which I could see no light. Until at last, one day, Vincent came along and took my hand. I let go of the fight and the sun shined in.

If someone has a problem with that, that's their problem.

And as it so happened, no one was more prickled by our deviant ways than Vincent's own mom. Missouri to the core, she wears her Bible belt with pride. She was adamant that her eleven children call her "Mother" and attend Catholic school, where they would learn faith, morals, and that a man does not lie down with another man. Especially not with one of her sons.

Vincent's father deflected the subject with stoic silence, or at most, "Oh well, you know how

Mother feels." I think he was too much of a gentleman to make waves.

They have always treated me, Vincent's friend, with Midwest politeness.

Hoot had a different spin on things. As soon as word got out that the powers that be had granted Vincent and me the legal right to become each other's old ball and chain, he was knocking at our door, bursting with enthusiasm.

"We'll do the ceremony right out at the edge of your property, overlooking the valley," Hoot said. "And afterwards, we'll have a barbeque and a bonfire."

We were his gays and he had big plans for us. Vincent and I hadn't even talked about it yet, but as far as Hoot was concerned, it was a done deal. Of course we were going to get married. Isn't this what we'd been waiting for? His enthusiasm was contagious.

Vincent and I looked at each other and smiled. There was never a formal proposal from Vincent to me or from me to Vincent. Neither of us got down on one knee. But there, in our sunny Catskill kitchen, with a mountain man yammering on about some friend who had a barbeque truck, Vincent and I looked past Hoot and directly at each other and realized that we did indeed love each other.

Anyway, it would be easier to say yes to eternity together than to say no to Hoot.

A barbeque would be nice. Keep it simple. Down home. Pagan.

Of course if anything goes wrong, nasty weather, an unruly band member or bad shrimp, it will surely confirm that somebody up there does not approve.

My eighty-five-year-old mother on the other hand loves weddings in any form. It wouldn't have mattered if I decided to marry a ficus. Mom would be there to cry and say how beautiful we look together.

She may be little and old and a lady but she is by no means a little old lady. Mom grew up in an Italian neighborhood in Paterson, New Jersey in the '30s and '40s. She's as sharp as a tack and just as brassy. She power walks a mile a day, happily gambles away my inheritance on weekly casino bus outings with the seniors, and makes the best spaghetti sauce east of the Meadowlands.

And I have my mother to thank for my artistic side. Early in my childhood she recognized a certain spark in me and saw it as her duty to nurture it. Dad taught us to hunt and fish and get dirty. My mom made sure to tote me away to Greenwich Village art openings, Broadway shows and Chinatown. She wanted me to see that there was a world beyond the dirt trails. I was only eight years old when Mom finagled us backstage to meet Carol Channing opening night of *Hello, Dolly.* I have to say, Miss Channing was very sweet. She took the time to sign my program, and even had her security guard personally escort us out the door into the alley.

When my parents first bought the tree farm, they thought of it as a weekend getaway. Mom would stay home in New Jersey and make us boys get away. She relished her days of peace and quiet in the suburbs.

Recently Mom has come to enjoy an occasional weekend in the country. She appreciates the beauty of nature and I think in some way it helps her summon up my father's spirit. Now that we brothers have grown and each has a farmstead of his own, our dear mother spreads her weekend stays between us.

This was our lucky weekend.

"Are you going to get married in a church?" Mom asked as Vincent set out a cheese board and a wooden bowl full of Triscuits. "You can't get married in a church." She was thinking out loud. "What church would marry you?"

She was making it sound like we had leprosy.

When she paused to cheese a cracker I said, "We are not getting married in a church, Mom. We were thinking..."

I looked up at Vincent and smiled, trying to project a cheery confidence, fully aware of the fact that my sweet, generous mother was going to have to help finance this venture so it was critical that she see our vision.

"Vincent and I were thinking, what better place to get married than right here on our beautiful estate?"

Mom froze mid-cheese.

Always the actor, Vincent seized the momentary silence. He motioned his arm toward the horizon.

"With this gorgeous view as a backdrop!"

A rooster crowed, and somewhere a dog was barking. My mother waved away a yellow jacket.

"An outdoor wedding?" She smiled but you could see in her eyes that we might as well have suggested skydiving off Mount Rushmore. "Your cousin had an outdoor wedding."

"Yes mom, I remember. I was best man. And it was beautiful."

She shrugged. "It rained."

I frowned. "For ten minutes at seven in the morning. Otherwise it was a perfect day."

She armed herself with a wedge of smoked Gouda.

"You never know with outdoor weddings. You're taking a big chance with the weather. Especially up here." The way she said *up here* implied *up here in Siberia*.

Vincent tried to placate her with a cup of tea and an assurance.

"We're going to rent a huge tent."

Vincent is like my mother's favorite daughter-in-law. He can sell her on anything. He spoke softly and calmly.

"We can even rent heaters, if you think it's a good idea, Mom."

He calls her Mom.

She groaned but her shoulders softened. After all, an outdoor wedding was, at least, a wedding.

Then I took the sales pitch one step too far.

"And we'll rent port-a-johns."

She spit her Gouda into a napkin and waved her hand in the air.

"It's none of my business. You do what you want. I'm going to keep my nose out of it. But I think it's a terrible idea. In a field?"

"It's a lawn." I said.

"A lawn full of chicken poop. Where is the altar going to be?"

Vincent put his arm on Mom's shoulder and motioned toward the view. She shook her head and pursed her lips. She was going to stay out of it.

"Where will the center aisle be?" she asked.

Vincent handed it off to me.

"Mom," I said, "there isn't going to be a center aisle."

"No aisle? There has to be an aisle! People won't know where to walk. People have to walk down an aisle. People *expect* to walk down an aisle. Your Aunt Josie will want to walk down an aisle. I want to walk down an aisle. There has to be an aisle!"

I tried to remain calm. I really tried.

"Mom, it's not a traditional wedding," I said. "We're two guys getting married. It's in no way traditional. It's a gathering of friends and family. Try to imagine it as a beautiful garden party."

I said "garden party" but Mom heard "bumpkin calamity".

Fortunately at that moment there was a knock at the door. It was Hoot wanting to borrow the pry bar. I think it was his pry bar to begin with, but it had been borrowed back and forth so many times the lines of ownership had become blurred.

Hoot joined us on the back deck. When he saw my mother he quickly took off his flap-eared hat and nodded. One didn't see Hoot with his hat off too often. Not a bad-looking guy, rugged but clipped, a head like a boulder.

"Pardon me," he bowed. "Didn't know you had company."

Really? You didn't see the Cadillac in the driveway?

"Mom, you remember our neighbor Hoot," Vincent said. Mom smiled and sort of stood up but then didn't.

Hoot grabbed her hand but didn't know what to do with it.

"Hoot. Hoot LeShea."

My mother was, of course, polite but she clearly didn't speak Mountain.

"Yes. How are you?"

Hoots eyes darted between us. He could sense he had walked in on something. To break the tension he suddenly pointed his fingers like two pistols.

"So, your two boys here tell you the big news?"

Mom blushed with pride.

"Yes, it's very exciting." Then she glanced toward the yard. "Right out there. In the weather."

Hoot dropped down into the chair right next to my mom with his camo pants and his big boots. Mom looked at him as if he were a raccoon that had just crawled out from under the porch. Hoot puffed out his jaw.

"My friend Swifty rents tents."

"Well," Mom said and then took a sip of Constant Comment, "you'll have to give me Swifty's phone number."

Okay, this was good. Give Mom a project.

"Yeah Mom," I said. "You can be in charge of talking to Swifty."

Mom glared at me over her tea cup. She knew my ulterior motive. She taught me ulterior motives.

"Sure thing," Hoot said. "Gonna be real. Can't beat the setting."

Mom shrugged and looked at me but spoke to Hoot.

148

"They're not going to have an aisle."

"Huh? No aisle?" Hoot scowled at me. "I don't want to get in your business but I gotta tell you, I'm with Mom on this one. You gotta have an aisle."

My mother smiled at Hoot and nudged his knee. They had formed an alliance. He called her Mom. But then Hoot noticed that I wasn't having it so he changed the subject.

"Anyways, when you fellows planning to throw this hoedown?"

"Hoedown?" I said.

"You can't wait too long," Mom sighed. "It will be too cold."

"We were thinking sometime in July," Vincent said.

Mom shook her head.

"July is awful."

Hoot said, "July is no good."

"It can be so hot," Mom said. "And people travel in July."

Hoot shook his head at the very thought.

"Fine, August then," I offered.

Mom held up a hand.

"Now hold on. Not too late in August. The nights can get cold."

"Don't have it in November," Hoot said. "That's bow season."

"We'll have it at the beginning of August," Vincent said as he scrolled on his phone. "Saturday, August ninth."

My mother nodded. It seemed like that might work. Hoot looked at his wristwatch even though he wasn't wearing one.

"Yep, I can do August nine."

"It's settled then," I said. "August ninth it is."

Right about then Neil came strolling around the corner.

"What's August ninth?" Neil asked as if he had just arrived late for a meeting.

"The boys are getting married," Hoot said. "Right'chere. August nine."

"Cool," Neil said. "Works for me."

Hoot turned to Mom.

"My friend Donnie Mootz owns the Hog Wild Barbeque Truck. Best pulled pork in the entire valley."

"You should get one of those bouncy castles," Neil said.

I assured him there would be no bouncy castle.

Mom stared out at the lawn and sighed.

"People expect to walk down an aisle."

14.

He woke us in the middle of the night.

I was probably only nine years old, but I remember it like it was yesterday. My dad, my two brothers and I were spending a winter weekend in the Catskills. Only on rare occasions did we venture upstate this time of year. The days were short and cold, the nights long and cold and the old farmhouse poorly insulated, if at all. By October my dad would have shut down the water and drained the pipes. There were no computers back then and the farmhouse didn't have a television or even a phone. In winter, our farm was a lonely place.

But this odd weekend Dad needed a break from his sales job. "A quick overnight," he told Mom. "Just to check on things."

She knew the farm was his secret lover, and she told us to go.

The summer bedrooms were as cold as meat lockers so we all slept in the den on an odd collection of 1950's lounge chairs and love seats left by some past inhabitants, now assembled in a half circle, wagon train style around a blazing wood stove.

Winter nights in the Catskills are black. I was deep in my sleeping bag in a fetal clutch around my pillow, safely hidden in my flannel cocoon, willing to stay there until May if need be.

I heard the back door open and heavy boots knocking snow onto the kitchen floor. My dad always did that. He must have been out gathering firewood.

I didn't move, just listened as he walked into the room. His footsteps approached and suddenly his strong hand shook my shoulder.

"Wake up, boys." Dad's voice was hushed but charged.

We brothers struggled to comprehend, annoyed when Dad switched on a lamp. My little brother was only six. He tried to roll away, to keep sleeping, but Dad pulled him back.

"Come on. Get up. Where are your boots?"

My older brother said, "What's going on?"

"Get your coat and hat. Help your brothers."

Dad held the back door open and we filed out.

We crossed through an alien landscape, the orchard on a winter night. A few shriveled apples stubbornly clung to the skeletal branches, deer tracks in the snow like Morse code for who had been there. It was strange and exciting to be in our heavy coats, hats, boots and pajamas.

The full moon and Milky Way reflected off the snow and lit up the night like I'd never seen before, or since. The ember end of Dad's cigarette was the single dot of orange in a phthalo blue world.

"It's so bright out here, you could read a book," my older brother said.

My younger brother stopped and stood in Dad's tracks.

"I'm cold."

"This way." Dad picked him up and carried him over the stone wall.

We followed, trudging through a thicket of huckleberry and up into the steep woods until at last we crested a clearing, a craggy outcropping we called Lookout Rock.

We stared out over the vast yawning valley. Dad pointed but he didn't need to. On the horizon neon green lights danced and whipped across the sky. A dazzling display that seemed like a celebration, or a battle, was happening in some far-off land.

"What is it, Daddy?" my younger brother asked.

"The Northern Lights," Dad said.

"Aurora Borealis," my older brother said. "I didn't know we got them here."

Without warning and as silent as mist, the ribbons of light suddenly flared up and splayed across the heavens directly above us.

"Wow," was all I could say.

At that moment I could feel that there were worlds beyond my little world, other peoples and other places beyond and beyond and beyond.

It was also at that moment that I realized that this was where I belonged, in my pajamas in the snow with my brothers and my dad.

If only I could hang onto it forever. Writing is the only way I know how.

The lights writhed and danced for another hour until they finally slunk away.

A glowing speck in the night was the farmhouse and the promise of a warm sleeping bag by the fire.

15.

There could be no more delaying it. The kitchen floor sagged and I couldn't shake the image of friends and family on our wedding day falling through the floor, next stop China.

The solution was simple. Jack up the house from underneath. Remove the rotten beam and replace it with a new one. Then put the house back down again. Simple.

I'm not talking about jacking the house up in the air like a fire tower. At most it would be lifted an inch, if even, just enough to take the weight off the old beam. That said, I don't want to make light of it either. You are lifting an eleven ton house over your head.

I had one jack, a big old greasy clunker that had been left behind in one of our sheds by the previous homeowner. It looked like it had seen some action in its day. Apparently jacking up houses to replace rotten beams is a regular Catskill pastime. This thing looked like it could right the Leaning Tower of Pisa. But you need two jacks. So Neil said he would bring one.

I had all the power tools and electric saws set out on the front lawn with the big new beam laid out, ready for duty. I was down in the crawl space beneath the house when Neil arrived. He crouched at the open basement window, blocking the sunlight.

"Whoa... spooky place," he said.

I had carefully assessed the situation. I knew exactly how we were going to proceed.

"You bring the jack?"

Neil reached into his jacket and brought forth a scrawny contraption of intertwined metal. It looked like a kid's Erector Set. I stared blankly.

"What?" Neil said.

"I thought you had a jack."

"It works." He pumped the little crank. It squeaked.

"We're jacking up a house. That thing couldn't lift a shoe box."

Neil wriggled his leggy self in through the tiny window, brushed away some dirt and set the little jack down on a flat rock.

"It's from Joey T's old Malibu."

"You can man that one. But I'm telling you if it falls apart...." I shook my head. "Okay, here's what we need to do."

I walked Neil through the plan. He listened intently, carefully scrutinizing the under-structure of the house. At one point Neil interrupted me and made a very good suggestion that I have to say actually would make the process easier. He was a clod but he did possess an innate clarity at understanding how things are put together. Then I noticed him staring wide-eyed into the shadows.

"Oh- my- god-," he said as he grabbed my shoulders. "Is that...? Is that a human skull?!"

I squinted, adjusting my eyes to the darkness.

"It's a light socket and a broken bulb."

"Oh." Neil slowly released his grip. "You might be right."

Neil crouched his way over to the far side of the crawl space and cleared a spot for his jack on the dirt floor.

"Brolsma's had a human skull in their basement."

I placed a thick wooden post on top of my jack and maneuvered it into position under an overhead beam.

"Nobody would go down that cellar for two years," Neil said as he took a post and got his jack into position. "Turned out to be an old Halloween mask."

"You ready?" I asked. "We'll stay together. And go slow."

Neil nodded and turned to face the task.

We both started cranking. Too fast at first. We slowed down as the jacks pushed up on the joists. A couple more cranks and there was a sudden SNAP!

We froze.

Everything was quiet and still.

"Okay," Neil whispered.   "That was just the house. It's going up."

Very slowly, almost timidly we both began to crank again. Another SNAP! And a CRACK! The framework groaned as the old house was being freed from its fieldstone foundation. We paused.

"Okay," I said. "On three. A little bit more. Ready...? One...two...three...."

We both cranked. There was a PING! Another crank and SNAP! Once more and POP! Then footsteps over head. We stopped. Vincent called out from above.

"What are you guys doing down there?"

"Nothing," I called back. "It's good. Everything's good."

Neil smiled a crooked grin as we waited for Vincent's reply.

"Well be careful," Vincent finally said. "I'm going downtown. Taking the little car. And Poke."

"Okay. Have fun," I called out. "We're out of shaving cream. Get the good stuff."

With Vincent leaving, Neil and I could focus on the job. We cranked the jacks once, twice, three times more.

SNAP! CRACKLE! POP!

Finally, a thin gap appeared between the rotten beam and the rest of the house above us. Neil and I were very proud of ourselves but there was no time to celebrate. Eleven tons of house was now free of its sill and suspended over our heads supported only by an old greasy clunker and the little jack from Joey T's Malibu.

"Okay, we need to get this rotten beam out of here and the new one in as quickly as we can." I grabbed a pry bar.

Neil just used his bare hands. He pulled and yanked at the decayed wood. It crumbled and chunks fell to the ground.

"It's like tuna," Neil said. "No wonder your kitchen sags."

I gathered up all the biggest pieces and tossed them out through the little casement window onto the front lawn.

"I got to talk to you about something," Neil said as he brushed a sprinkle of black carpenter ants off his shoulder. "It's kind of very important."

That sounded odd coming from Neil. I didn't know what to say.

"I got to go to New Mexico," he said.

"Huh?"

"I got to go meet Natalie. We been talking for a long time now. I got to talk to her for real."

"But Neil... are you sure she's who she says she is?"

"I got to go. I got to."

I suddenly felt older and wiser, ready to guide this young lad in the ways of the world. I opened my mouth to speak but then didn't. The look in his eyes silenced me. I had seen that look before. I know that look well.

The look of Clyde.

When I was a kid in New Jersey the Lagatuda family lived directly across the cul-de-sac from us. The Lagatuda boys were trouble times five. They skipped school to smoke pot and cigarettes in their backyard. They shot B.B. guns at beer bottles and kept an ever evolving pack of mongrel dogs. They were forever having unplanned litters of puppies birthed in their garage or underneath the back porch. The Lagatudas idea of spay and neuter was to just keep the dogs separated. It worked. Sometimes.

One day Sheba, the pack's subordinate young female, came into heat.

The Lagatuda boys sequestered Sheba inside a six foot high chain link kennel at the far end of their property. They also took the added precaution of chaining Clyde, the pack's alpha male, to his plywood doghouse at the far other end of their property. Clyde was one tough dog. It may be urban legend, but people say that he was half bull mastiff and half hyena. And I believe it. Just to be safe the boys also looped Clyde's chain through two cinder blocks and the steel axle off an F-250.

That took care of that.

Clyde sniffed at the air and tested his chain. He had that look in his eyes.

It was summer and everyone slept with their windows open. Throughout that night and into the wee hours the entire neighborhood was serenaded by the plaintive wailing of poor love sick Clyde. His heartbreaking howls drifted on the warm night air, blending with the sweet erotic scent of bitch in heat.

In the morning our cul-de-sac buzzed with the news that Clyde had scaled the kennel fence and was hanging by his chain. During the night he managed to drag his now collapsed doghouse, the two cinder blocks and the axle across the entire back property, leaving a long jagged furrow of plowed sod in his wake. He then somehow climbed the six foot fence and was now lynched by his neck with his hind legs barely touching the ground. The Lagatuda boys cut his chain just in the nick of time. Clyde was immediately locked in the garage where he slept for the next four days.

Two months later, Sheba snuck under the back porch, dug out a shallow trough in the dry dirt, and gave birth to seven healthy puppies. They looked like they were part hyena.

Never underestimate the look of Clyde.

"Anyway," I said to Neil. "How are you going to get there?"

"Ah," he smiled, "that's where you come in."

"I am not driving to New Mexico."

"No," he said. "I'm going to buy your truck."

"You want to buy that rusted-out hunk of junk?"

"Why not?" he said. "The frame is solid. And it's dependable and good on gas."

I thought about it. "Okay, four thousand dollars."

"For that rusted-out hunk of junk?!"

"Why not?" I said. "The frame is solid. And it's dependable and good on gas."

With great effort we managed to wrestle the new beam into position and with a nod at each other we simultaneously released the pressure valves. The jacks hissed and the mass of house settled back down with a mighty groan. It now sat proud and strong on a firm new sill. It would be good for a long long time. Neil and I high fived each other for a job well done. We even took a moment to scrawl out a time capsule message on the beam in pencil.

I wrote, *"To you of the future... Forgive us for our mistakes. May you have learned from them and prospered."* And then I wrote the date.

Neil wrote, *"Your a butthead."*

I set up shop on the front lawn to cut the boards that secure the spaces between the joists. Neil would pop his head out the crawlspace window and shout out the measurements. I cut the boards to his specifications and tossed them in through the window and he nailed them into position.

"Twenty three and five eighths by eleven and a quarter!"

He was very precise. No two were alike. I cut the board to the length with the miter saw and trimmed it off on my table saw.

"Twenty four and a quarter by eleven and a half!"

As the table saw whirred its way along the pencil line I got lost in my thoughts.

Funny guy, Neil, with his crooked smile and his Clyde eyes. Maybe I should sell him my truck. I really do need a new one. I could give him a good deal.

There is a hard and fast rule when using power saws: PAY ATTENTION. That's why it happened. I hate to even think about it but it did happen. I was guiding the board along the blade with my left hand, pushing with my right, my mind a million miles away when- *ZSHUNGGG!*

I cut the tip off my left index finger.

Time stood still. Nothing existed. Not my house, not Neil, not Vincent, not my mother, not the universe. I was staring at a searing glaring terrifying reality: my finger, missing the end. A perfect severed cut of red flesh and white bone. I could see my bone! And then blood!

"NEIL!" I screamed. "COME QUICK! I CUT MY FINGER! BAD!"

I clutched my left hand in my right and held them into my stomach. I couldn't look at it again.

Neil sprung out of that crawl space like a jackrabbit. He grabbed my hands and pulled them into view. He took a quick assessment then pushed my hands back into my stomach.

"Don't move," he said. "I'll be right back."

He ran into the house.

"Neil! Neil!"

I staggered after him, dripping blood. Lots of blood. My blood. My mind was racing.

This isn't happening! This isn't me! This is some other guy!

Then I stopped and turned back.

I have to find the tip!

On the lawn. Somewhere in the grass. But there were chips of wood and sawdust everywhere.

How will I find it? No time. No time. But I have to!

Suddenly the tip came into focus. There it was on the ground beneath the saw. A small pink chunk of me. A tiny white speck of bone. Staring back at me like the Devil's eye. I grabbed it up and stumbled into the house. Drip. Drip. Drip. Blood on the foyer floor.

"Neil!"

I reached for the truck keys.

Neil ran at me from the kitchen. He shoved a bag of frozen French fries over my wounded hand. The cold immediately numbed the pain. He pushed me toward the door.

"Let's go!"

"Wait- wait!" I suddenly realized something. "The tip! I dropped the tip!"

"What?! Where?!"

Felt like I was going to pass out. I wobbled around in an aimless circle, like someone who just got off a bad carnival ride.

"I- I don't know... somewhere."

Neil quickly zigzagged over the front lawn like a hunting dog.

"Here it is!"

He pulled the keys from me and handed me the fingertip.

"Don't lose it! Now go!"

Neil pushed me toward the truck. I opened the passenger side door and fell into the seat. I leaned into my knees and rocked back and forth. Neil ran around and jumped into the driver seat. He shoved the keys into the ignition.

"Ut-oh," he said.

I was fading fast. Spinning.

"Wha- What?"

Neil had a pathetic look on his face.

"I don't know how to drive a stick."

I slumped forward and groaned.

"I thought you wanted to buy this truck. Owww! Push down on the clutch!"

"I'll figure it out." Neil turned the key. The truck lurched forward and stalled. "Which one is the clutch?"

Drip. Drip. Drip. Blood trickled onto my crotch.

"Ohhhh... hurry!"

Neil started the truck again and shoved it into reverse. But it rolled forward and knocked over the garbage cans. He slammed on the brakes. Grinding the gears, he searched for reverse. Finally he got us turned around and on our way. I just rocked back and forth breathing through my teeth, begging him to hurry.

"Let up on the clutch and give it some gas. Ooooowww....."

The little truck bounced and skidded down Laurel Lane making a horrible grinding sound every time Neil forced it into a different gear.

Viola Dink was standing out near the end of the road picking boysenberries as we flew by. She half waved, not sure what to make of our obvious panic. We covered her in a cloud of red dust.

You have no idea how far the ten miles to town is until you cut off the end of your finger. Neil was getting the hang of shifting gears, speeding along the reservoir with me rocking back and forth, gasping and groaning.

"Push on the clutch... put it in fourth... ease up slowly!"

"It's okay," Neil said. "You'll be okay." He put his hand on my shoulder.

I have to tell you, if you ever find yourself in an emergency situation, touch the person who needs help. It really is comforting, the simple touch from a fellow human being.

We crested over a hill and straight at a herd of deer. We both screamed. Neil yanked the steering wheel. The truck veered off the road. The deer scattered. We bounced over a grassy berm and skidded back onto the road.

To chill the pain I pressed down on the bag of frozen French fries folded over my hand. It was quick thinking on Neil's part, except for the fact that French fries look like fingers. I was writhing in the seat, moving my legs and rocking back and forth, anything to distract me from my finger. With my good hand I clicked open the glove compartment and dug around for something to put the tip into, finally settling on a Jeff Bank envelope.

They weren't able to reattach the tip but they assured me that fingers are very good at regenerating from injury, though the nail may never grow back.

I was lucky that the doctor on duty in the emergency room knew all about missing body parts. As he stitched my finger he comforted me with a few horror stories. The nurse also chimed in with a nightmarish tale about her Uncle Sal and the lawn mower and his toes. That's the thing when you lose a finger tip. For the rest of your life you are treated to an endless stream of ghoulish tales about everybody's uncle or cousin or friend who lost a finger, a hand or a toe.

Neil sat swiveling in a chair, eating the French fries right out of the bag.

"I'm going have to start calling you Stubby." He bit a fry in half.

"You do realize those aren't cooked," I said.

I was stretched out on an examination chair, a roll of white paper crinkled beneath me, my finger swathed in bandages, my shirt and pants soaked in blood, pain killers making everything just fine.

Then we heard a familiar voice and suddenly the curtain was pulled back. Vincent looked down at me and smiled.

"It's always something with you."

His embrace made me whole again.

One month later all the neighbors gathered in our yard to bid farewell to Neil.

My new silver truck was parked in the driveway and Neil had Rusty loaded down with all his worldly possessions, which wasn't very much.

Everyone was hugging Neil and shaking his hand and wishing him good luck. Viola Dink even baked him a banana mushroom pie for the road. Though he didn't approve of Neil leaving, Uncle Hoot knew there was no stopping him.

"Sorry I'm going to miss the big event," Neil said, pointing to Stephanie's now showing belly.

"You be careful out there," Hoot said. "Don't be stupid, knucklehead."

Hoot pulled Neil into a hug. Man to man. No one dared notice the quivering corners of Hoot's mouth.

I held up the keys.

"Hey you never paid me the fifty bucks." Turned out Neil was a shrewd bargainer.

"I'll mail it to you when I get a pay check," he promised. Then with a crooked smile he said, "You be careful, Stubby. I'm not going to be here to watch after you."

Then we hugged. I really was going to miss that goofball. I handed Neil the keys.

"Go get 'em, Clyde."

Neil climbed into the truck and shut the door. Then with a quick nod, mountain style, Neil and Rusty drove off down the lane, gears grinding, muffler belching.

"I don't think he's going to make it to New Mexico," Ross said.

"I don't think he's going to make it to the mail boxes," Hoot said.

There was one final backfire BOOM, as Neil turned left onto the road that lead to the highway and to the rest of his life.

"He'll make it," I smiled. "He'll make it."

16.

I was driving my new truck, Silverbird, through the back roads on my way home from somewhere. The thing about living in the country, everything is a distance away, friends, work, doctors, groceries. But having no traffic makes the endless ribbons of winding roads magic to explore. I sped along through the hills, Poke at my side.

Never been back here before, but I think it comes out by the Claryville Bridge.

Then up ahead, a hand painted sign forced my foot to the brake.

"Barn Sale".

At forty miles an hour I can tell whether or not a road side sale is worth stopping for. If you see lots of clothes or kids toys don't even slow down. Yard Sale trumps Garage Sale and Barn Sale trumps them both. And a hand painted sign...

I turned onto the dirt driveway and drove slowly past a proud white farmhouse of Wyeth beauty. A massive sugar maple shaded the backyard where a 1960s swing set sat in idle rust. At the edge of the mowed lawn, beyond a stone fence, a sunny pasture where cows must have once grazed was now overgrown with Timothy and Golden Rod.

There was a huge red barn with its doors propped open and a treasure trove of country furnishings sprawled out in a beckoning display.

I thought no one was around. Then a big old dog lumbered out into the sun and squinted his cataract eyes at us. With great effort he woofed a muffled woof. But even he knew his threatening bravado was a thing of the past. Poke's paws were on the dashboard, her tail wagging out, "New friend! New friend! New friend!"

And then a man appeared at the open doors. He was old and bent. He, too, squinted through cataract eyes. I parked the truck and told Poke to stay.

"Hello," I said as I approached the old man.

"Hello back," he said as he propped a wooden croquet set against a Windsor chair. "Most everything's marked. If you don't see a price just ask."

His face was lined by a life lived. A thin scar above his eye could tell a story.

"She can come out and say hello." He nodded toward Poke.

"Oh well, she...."

There was no use arguing. Poke knew what he said. I opened the truck door and the two dogs greeted each other like old friends and then headed off to explore.

I spied a set of old tools in a wooden box.

"You're selling these?"

They were beautiful, well worn but well cared for. The old man shrugged.

"Don't need them where I'm going."

I lifted out a rolled canvas pouch of chisels, their handles polished smooth by years of service.

"North Carolina. Don't get the winters. Be near the grandchildren."

"I'll give you twenty bucks for these."

He looked at my new truck.

"Thirty and we got a deal."

I carefully placed the tool box to one side then turned my attention to three bushel baskets neatly stacked with Mason jars, real ones, with tiny chips and scuffed glass. They had seen many seasons of preserves.

"How much for these?"

The old man glanced up at the porch. That's when I noticed the old woman, sitting in a wheelchair, just watching with a smile as soft as her apron. The man hushed his voice.

"Give me fifteen. And you can take the baskets too."

I was excited about that. Vincent and I were planning to give away little perennial flower plants at our wedding. These jars would make perfect containers.

"That's a deal. I'll use them for centerpieces on the tables. I'm getting married next month."

The old man smiled.

"Oh, a local girl?"

I reached for my wallet and counted out the bills.

"Not exactly."

I tried to give him the money but he held up his hands.

"Not me. Give it to the boss." He smiled toward the old woman.

I walked over and stepped up to her. Her white hair was tied back away from her sweet face. I could tell that at one time, she must have been quite attractive. I handed her the money.

"Here you go. Forty five dollars."

"Thank you."

She took the money and folded it into her apron pocket though I don't think she knew exactly why I was handing it to her.

The old man stepped up behind her.

"Better count it twice, sweetie. He's a shifty fella." He winked at me.

The old woman just smiled and nodded her head. The man brushed back her hair.

"You know what they say, young man, happy wife, happy life."

Then he gave his wife a squeeze and nuzzled into her neck. She cooed but pushed him away.

"You are trouble, Henry Bender."

On the road again, Poke and I rolled through the hills. I was quite proud of my purchases. I couldn't wait to show Vincent the amazing set of tools. He was going to love the jars. They couldn't be more perfect.

I wondered if Vincent and I would be like that couple one day, still together but with a life behind us, selling off our tools, moving to North Carolina.

Maybe. If we're lucky.

The road did finally cross over the Claryville Bridge and I was back on familiar turf. I stopped at the mailboxes and ours was quite stuffed, the usual bills but also three more RSVPs and a package from our friends Nicki and Louisa. Our first wedding present!

I let Poke out there and she followed Silverbird the rest of the way down Laurel Lane. Vincent was in the front yard, toiling in the garden on his hands and knees, digging in the dirt with a trowel and a bucket. He smiled up at me.

"I'm thinning out all these lilies." He dug the trowel into the earth and pulled at the tangled roots. "They'll be perfect for the giveaways."

"And wait until you see what I have!"

I walked around the back of the truck and retrieved one of the baskets of jars. I turned to Vincent but he was preoccupied, digging still, almost feverishly.

When you know a person so well, you just know when something is wrong. I can tell Vincent's moods by the back of his head.

Something was wrong.

"Look." I held out the basket.

But Vincent couldn't see. There was dirt smudged around his eyes. He smiled but his words came out in quakes.

"I spoke to my parents today."

"Oh." I put the basket back in the truck. "Are they coming to the wedding?"

I asked, though I knew the answer.

Vincent just shook his head and kept digging.

"I had to know why they didn't respond to our invitation," he said. "I had to hear it from them." He stabbed at the ground. "My father just made excuses but my mother grabbed the phone from him and yelled, 'Marriage is between a man and a woman!' Then she hung up. I tried to call back but they wouldn't answer."

He was digging way more lilies than we would ever need. I went to him and put my hand on his. He stopped digging and began to cry. I held him. Of course I did. Vincent was never much of a crier but he sure cried now.

"They just ignored us, Scott."

"I know. I know."

It was all I could say. In his deepest sorrow, I felt my deepest love.

"And you wonder why I drank." He stabbed the earth again. "I haven't had a drink for almost two months."

"I know."

"But today I was going to. After they hung up on me, I was so mad I thought about getting in the car and driving to town and buying a big bottle of wine. To hell with them."

Vincent stood up and dropped the shovel into the pail.

"But then I said no." He wiped the dirt from his knees. "No. I am not going to let them do this."

I let Vincent finish his thoughts. I looked straight into his eyes and brushed back his hair.

"I love you, Vincent. And you and I are going to get married."

17.

It was a circus and Hoot was the ringleader.

A big truck maneuvered into the backyard and a crew of guys unloaded port-o-johns and assembled a gigantic tent. Hoot knew what went where and why.

Our wedding was just a few days out and some of the guests had already arrived. Three of Vincent's sisters drove in from Missouri and pitched tents in the orchard. It was shaping up to be a mini Woodstock. Mom had commandeered the guest room and was barking orders-- I'm sorry, making excellent suggestions on how things should be set up.

"How are ladies going to walk around if they are wearing high heels?" she wondered. "We need to roll out some red carpets."

She and Hoot made an unlikely, yet incredibly effective duo. Mom got Vincent and two of his sisters to tackle stringing up lights. Hoot assigned another sister to mow the lawn. I was mostly in charge of checking the weather reports and worrying. It seemed like every time I logged onto my computer the little graphic for RAIN on our wedding day was darker and more intense. One website even flashed little bolts of lightning.

I decided to find something to distract myself for awhile and wandered out into the yard. Poke was excited by all the strangers and activity. It was like a movie set. Everyone had a job to do. Honestly, I felt a bit useless.

"You okay?" Hoot asked.

I snapped out of my daze.

"Yeah. Sure. Just looking around."

Hoot studied my face. A sly smile came to his.

"Not getting buck fever, are you?"

A couple of tent guys snickered but it was actually an inside joke between Hoot and me.

It had been many months but obviously Hoot wasn't going to let me forget that day. He punched me on the shoulder and exaggerated the words.

"Buck fever."

Five A.M. Opening Day of bow season arrived cold and dark. I met Hoot, as planned, around the back of his trailer. We spoke in whispers because that's what hunters do and because Stephanie was sleeping in the trailer.

For some reason I got this idea in my head that I wanted to join Hoot on a deer hunt.

As a kid, back on the tree farm, I did some hunting. Cottontails and squirrels mostly, maybe an occasional woodchuck, but never big game, never a deer. I had to try it, to see what it was all about, to experience it for myself, like a real man.

I bought full camo gear, arrows and a bow. I have to say, I looked smashing.

For months I practiced almost every day in the backyard with a paper bull's-eye stapled to a hay bale. I honed my skills to the point where from twenty five yards away, I could hit the hay bale.

Hoot was impressed that I actually showed up. He too was in full camo. Even his face was rubbed with camo colors. He strapped a small but intense headlight around his flap-eared hat.

Being a seasoned pro, Hoot had a compound bow that was a masterpiece of trapezoid engineering, a perfectly balanced assembly of finely tuned levers and pulleys. I bought my bow at Rite-Aid.

Hoot sniffed the air around me.

"Didn't shower, did you? Deer smells soap, thinks man."

"Nope. Haven't showered for three days now."

"Good." He handed me a little compact of camo make-up. "Here. Do your face." I used the side mirror on Hoot's pick-up.

There were suddenly bright lights as another truck drove up Laurel Lane and slowed to a stop. They rolled down the passenger side window. It was too dark to make out who it was. Just a man's voice.

"Hey Hoot. Where you guys heading?"

Hoot didn't look up. He was focused on precisely adjusting the tension on his bow.

"Other side of Harley's cornfield. You?"

"Down by Bender's Creek."

We knew they weren't going down by Bender's Creek. Just as they knew we weren't going to the other side of Harley's cornfield. Opening Day is a chess game.

Hoot nodded. "Good luck."

I said good luck also, but it sounded kind of weird.

"You guys too," the guy said.

The air crackled with anticipation. The truck drove off.

In unison Hoot and I mounted our ATVs. Hoot's was a big honking machine, camo painted and mud splattered. I borrowed Stephanie's ATV. It was a whole size smaller than Hoot's but nice new tires and the fenders were a pretty shade of lilac. We revved the engines. Hoot nodded to me.

"Stick together."

It was game on.

We headed up the old logging trail. My hands were freezing cold but I didn't want to stop and search my pockets for my gloves. No time now. About a mile up we turned off the trail and into the woods. I followed Hoot's halo of light as it flashed along the forest floor. Now and then my ATV would hit a root or a rock and jerk to one side but I managed to keep up. Neither of us spoke, but we both had one thing on our minds. Big George.

Big George is a magnificent whitetail buck who has eluded hunters in these mountains for the past eleven years. A noble stag, Big George is only ever seen on Opening Day. Then he vanishes deep into the wilderness, beyond the range of humankind. They say he is descended from the Great Adirondack Herd. They say he outweighs most local bucks by fifty pounds. They say he plays mind games with those who try to hunt him.

We crossed down into a steep ravine and up the other side. At last we came to an old stone foundation where we ditched the ATVs and continued on foot. We took a shortcut through the Hahn's cow pasture. The cows stared at us with dull curiosity. Not often do they have human visitors crossing their pasture at this ungodly hour. Hoot told me to keep an eye out for the bull. I was pretty sure he was kidding. But I kept an eye out just the same.

We each held the barbed wire down for the other guy as we left the open pasture and entered a deep dark forest of old growth hemlock. Now we slowed down our pace. Three thoughtful steps, then stop. Wait. Three more steps. Stop again. The carpet of hemlock needles underfoot made each step moccasin quiet.

We finally reached the edge of a stone outcropping that, at sunrise, would present an uninterrupted view of the valley floor. Unspoiled scenery that hasn't changed since the time of the Mohicans.

"This is the place," Hoot whispered. "This is where I saw Big George."

Hoot and I hunkered down against a massive tree trunk. Its roots embraced us like armchairs. Hoot faced south. I faced east. In the dark we waited.

And waited.

A shimmer of daylight quaked on the horizon. Veils of fog floated down from the warm waters of the reservoir and haunted the cold valley below. It was November so most of the leaves had fallen. But thickets of mountain laurel and wild rhododendron remained.

Far far off, somewhere in the hills a little family pack of coyotes chortled, howled and yipped at the dawn of a new day.

"This is the life, eh Hoot?"

Hoot smirked.

"Beats a desk job."

There are doctors, bankers, scientists and poets but I have just as much respect for Hoot, perhaps more. Some men analyze the stock exchange, others map the human genome. Hoot can read the tracks of animals and understand their movements and behavior. His skills as a woodsman are unparalleled. It was a great honor to be at his side in a deer hunt.

I wondered if the surrounding nature was having the same spiritual effect on both of us.

"What are you thinking about, Hoot?'

Hoot set his gaze on the distant slope.

"Dirty dishes."

I frowned. Hoot glanced at me and smiled.

"I figured out the secret to a happy life. You got to love washing dirty dishes."

I nodded yes, but I didn't know what the heck he was talking about.

"The way I see it," Hoot continued, "there are always dirty dishes to wash. No matter how much you wash them, there will always be more on the horizon. Life's an endless train of dirty dishes."

Hoot took out a small pair of binoculars and scanned the valley.

"If you want to live a happy life, learn to love washing dirty dishes."

Then he froze like a statue.

"There he is."

I sat up tall and strained to see what Hoot saw. Far down in the lower valley, through the blue haze of dawn I could just make out a small herd of deer. Maybe three. Grazing in the meadow. It looked like two does and a large buck.

Hoot focused the binoculars.

"That's him. That's him for sure. Big George." Hoot was a puma. "Enjoy your harem while you can, Your Majesty. Your reign is about to come to an end." He handed me the binoculars. "Have a look."

I put them to my eyes but I was breathing heavy and steamed up the lenses. It was like looking through Vaseline. I couldn't see a thing.

"Oh yeah," I lied.

"Big boy," Hoot said.

"Real big," I said.

Hoot hushed his voice. "Okay here's what we're gonna do."

We crouched low. Hoot held my shoulder with one hand and with the other he used a stick to scratch out a plan on the ground.

"You stay here. The deer are here. I'm gonna head out this way."

He scratched a big arch in the mossy earth.

"I'll make a real slow circle down and around."

I shook my head yes.

"Take our time. Nice and steady. If I can't get a clear shot myself, I'll drive them up and around through the pass, between the waterfall and the cliffs."

He paused to look over his shoulder, as if to make sure no one was eavesdropping.

"If all goes right, they should move up along here. I'll keep the pressure on and drive them _right_ _to_ _you_."

He pushed down on the stick and it snapped in two. I flinched.

"Okay," I nodded.

Hoot strapped his bow over his shoulder, patted me once on the back and descended the steep embankment, disappearing into a jungle of mountain laurel.

I just sat there.

All alone.

And waited.

I shivered, more from nerves than cold but the rising sun gave little warmth. The days are short this time of year and the sun was low in the sky, casting long cold shadows across the valley. I could still see the grazing deer, now at the edge of the tree line.

It was numbingly still. No sounds. Not a breeze. Not a chickadee.

And waited.

I felt a mystical connection to the past. Eons ago some indigenous hunter surely leaned against a tree at this same spot and gazed out at this same valley. The surrounding hills and forests exhaled with spirits.

I looked back to the meadow and the deer were gone.

They wouldn't really come this way... would they?

I carefully removed an arrow from my quiver, rolled it between my fingers, and studied the slender staff, its steely razor point waiting for its chance. A gleaming messenger of death.

I'm sure they won't come this way. But just in case....

Slowly, methodically I centered the nock of the arrow on the string and rested the shaft on the bow as I had so diligently practiced all summer.

I took a deep breath.

And waited.

My mind wandered. Pretty soon I was thinking about the Snickers Bar that was in my back pocket.

I was startled by a sudden *whoosh* as a bird flew overhead. I think it was a grouse. Made my heart race.

Which direction would they come from? If they did come? Which I highly doubt they will.

I adjusted my position and held the bow up, aimed toward the hillside.

And waited.

They could really go anywhere, in any direction. The options are limitless out here. What makes Hoot so sure he could drive them this way? Why would they come uphill and not head further down into the valley? I wonder if I have time to eat that Snickers Bar?

I decided to go for it. I held the bow and arrow awkwardly between my chin and shoulder and fumbled around in my back pocket for the candy bar. *Found it.* A bit smashed but certainly edible. I started tearing back the paper.

Then I heard a noise.

For one second I was torn between two priorities, the Snickers and the bow. I dropped the Snickers and lifted the bow into position.

I heard the noise again.

Off to the southeast. A rustle of leaves. A twig snap.

Then silence.

I aimed the arrow in that direction. A wall of mountain laurel.

Is it cold? Why am I shivering? What was that?

I pulled back on the string and tried to steady my aim but it trembled.

Footsteps on leaves.

Is it really a deer? Maybe it's Hoot. Maybe he's coming back.

More footsteps.

Coyotes? Coydogs? Psycho Pete?

I pulled back with all my strength. Blood surged through my veins. My ears were ringing.

It can't be the deer. It can't be. It--

--crashed through the laurels and into the little clearing directly in front of me. Startled and confused, the huge buck huffed and snorted and sucked the air. With a massive white chest and thick strong neck this wild creature was truly noble. Gleaming antlers crowned its proud head. There could be no doubting it.

This was Big George.

The point of my arrow was lined at his heart but shaking like a seismic needle.

Release. Release. Release.

For a moment, an infinitesimal everlasting moment, the great stag stared me down.

Do it! I can't! You have to! I can't! Do it now!

With a surging leap the buck pushed past me. I fell backwards. Released the arrow. It whizzed past the deer and lodged fifty feet above in the trunk of a sugar maple.

And the deer was gone.

I sat stunned for a moment, my fingers numb from holding the bow string. I heard a crackle of branches and Hoot came through at the same spot in the laurel. He looked flushed and briar scratched but his bow at the ready.

"Ya see him?!" he said. "Came this way! Did ya see him?!

I picked myself up off the ground and scraped the Snicker's Bar off my elbow. Hoot looked at me. Then up at the arrow in the tree, a permanent reminder of the one that got away.

Hoot's jaw dropped.

"You...? You...?"

"I... I..."

"You missed? You choked? You choked! "

"I... I..."

Hoot slapped his leg.

"Buck fever!" He burst out laughing. "You got buck fever!"

There is little a man can say when he stands exposed before the ranks. I could only hope that one day Hoot would forget about this little incident. He smacked me on the back.

"Buck fever!"

Hoot's laughter echoed through the valley.

And Big George lived to rule another day.

Hoot had the tent guys and Vincent's sisters laughing with his animated rendition of the event. He was pulling back on an imaginary bow string and shaking like an electric paint mixer.

I was about to state my case but was saved when Hoot's cell phone beeped a little banjo tune.

Hoot eyed his text message and immediately his demeanor changed. He held his phone out at arm's length and stared at it. A look of shock washed over his face.

"It's Stephanie," he said. "She..."

No one spoke.

"Her water... I got to go."

He staggered in a loopy circle.

"I got to go. It's Stephanie. I'm gonna be a dad. I'm gonna be a dad."

Hoot shook my hand, Vincent's hand, everybody's hand. We all wished him good luck and we turned him in the right direction and pushed.

"I'm gonna be a dad."

Hoot hurried home.

At 12:01 the next morning Daniel Lucas LeShea came into the world.

"Eight pounds, eleven ounces!"

Hoot couldn't have been prouder if he was talking about a bass.

August Nine

In the end the skies didn't crash down on us. In fact I have to say it was one of the prettiest days I have ever seen.

Guests arrived from far and wide. All ten of Vincent's siblings came armed with love.

When Stephanie and Hoot showed up with that new baby they were the hit of the wedding. Ever so tenderly Hoot lifted his newborn son from his wife's arms and handed him to Vincent.

"Daniel, meet your Uncles Scott and Vincent."

Hoot tugged the blanket away from the baby's face. The baby squirmed like a little pink mouse. Dressed in a camo onesie, he looked like a mini Hoot.

Best surprise of all, Neil and his girlfriend Natalie flew in for the weekend.

"On a jet," Neil said. "A 737. Freaky at first. But you get use to it. You just watch a movie. I had like six Cokes. In fact I got to hit those port-o-johns."

I have to say Neil looked dapper in khakis and new shoes, no more duct tape and his hair had been cut by an actual barber.

Natalie was sweet and bright and pretty and she had her arm locked on Neil.

"I'm working for Natalie's dad," Neil told everyone. "He owns a construction company. We build real stuff. Not like the amateur things Stubby and I used to do here." He flashed a crooked smile.

"Thank you," I said.

I was happy for Neil. That lanky lunk had finally grown into his boots. If I may jump ahead a few years, I can tell you that Neil stayed in New Mexico. He and Natalie got married and had two daughters. Neil and his father-in-law went on to become partners in a building company. They built award winning open-air plazas with shops and offices and townhouses. An article in the Albuquerque Journal said, "...developer Neil LeShea has single handedly enhanced the face of Downtown Las Cruces."

At some spontaneous moment a hush fell over the crowd. Vincent and I found ourselves standing alone together with the glorious Catskills behind us and our loved ones in front of us.

Our dear friend Peter cleared his throat and raised his hand and everyone fell silent and turned to face us.

Right then, as if by some force of magic, the guests suddenly divided into two groups and a perfect aisle was formed between them. My mother looked radiant in her lime green silk jacket, diamond earrings and bare feet as she strutted up the aisle arm and arm with Hoot to take her place beside us. She leaned in close and lovingly whispered to me.

"Stand up straight. You're slouching."

Mom could not have been more proud. Vincent turned and whispered to Hoot.

"Did you ever think you'd see the day?"

Hoot shook his head and smiled.

"World's turned upside down."

We were ready to begin.

When I lived in California I did a lot of camping. One weekend I went out to Joshua Tree and hiked way out into the desert. That night as I sat alone by my campfire, gazing up at the stars, I suddenly had an epiphany. I realized that I was all alone in life. My friends were all getting married, my brothers were married but I was alone and it seemed that always would be.

But it was okay. I liked myself. I had good friends and a loving family. And so I gave it up to the universe. That moment, alone in the desert, I made peace with myself and accepted my destiny. I poured my remaining bottled water on a little cactus plant, crawled into my tent and went to sleep.

The next morning I was amazed to see that the little cactus had burst into full bloom. I guess it was just waiting for water. I packed up my tent, hiked out of the desert and drove back to L.A.

That very day, while walking along Santa Monica Boulevard I bumped into a friend and he introduced me to Vincent. My very first impression was, "Wow, he has great hair. He must be very intelligent."

Here we are 15 years later.

Vincent makes me complete. He challenges and inspires me. He straightens my shirt collar, corrects my spelling and laughs at my jokes.

Marrying Vincent makes me come into full bloom.

There were some great laughs and lots of hugging.

My young nephew toasted that he didn't see what the big deal was, he had always thought of Uncle Vincent as part of the family.

Instead of a wedding cake, Viola Dink made twenty four pies! Twelve different flavors, including her now famous arugula butterscotch. Mm... my mouth waters.

When I bumped into Neil on the pie line I touched him on the shoulder.

"Hey man, thanks for coming."

"Wouldn't miss it."

"And thanks for the awesome gift."

"Didn't I tell you it would be a hit?"

Neil beamed with pride. Across the yard there was a lineup of excited guests waiting for their chance to jump around inside the bouncy castle.

In the evening we had a bonfire. There was a sing along and I heard that some people even went swimming in the pond. My high school friend Kathy and her husband Will came up the path laughing.

"There's a naked man in your woods!"

I quickly looked past them but of course I saw no one.

"Yeah," I sighed. "That's just Pete."

"Yes, he's a taxidermist," Kathy said. "He said to tell you congratulations."

Between the tents, the smoke, and the strumming guitars our wedding really had brought a little bit of Woodstock back to the Catskills.

Peace guided the planets and love steered the stars.

It was the best day of our lives.

*   *   *

It didn't take long to get back to normal and settle in to the rest of our days, or as I call them, the salad days.

With some wedding money we built a new deck. It turned out great and Vincent and I worked well together though I still keep looking for Neil.

The days are getting shorter now, and flocks of geese link across the sky.

A few days ago some animal got into our hen house and killed seven of our chickens. I'm going to have to set a trap. It could have been a raccoon or a mink. I'm not sure. Ross swears he saw a coydog spooking around.

I drove Silverbird down into the woods to get some firewood and tore the muffler off on a tree stump. Now it sounds like a tank. That poor truck is already starting to show some rust on the undercarriage. So many hassles.

Maybe it's like Hoot says; you just have to learn to love washing dirty dishes.

But the woods are beautiful today. Surrounded by nature I always feel my dad's presence. I looked up at the trees and took a moment to remember him.

Thanks Dad.

Just as I humped the last of the logs into the back of the truck I heard a noise. Like a man clearing his throat. Poke stood up and woofed. She was facing the thickets, her tail wagging.

"Hello," I called out. "Pete?"

A young couple stepped out. They were smartly dressed with expensive haircuts and they smelled good, like soap. I felt a bit grungy in my camo pants and big boots. They were very nice, the woman was quite attractive. They had a surveyors map and had just bought a piece of property down the lane. They were going to build a weekend place.

The guy said, "We're going to make our driveway come in along there." He pointed to the far side of Hoot's property. "You don't think that fellow would mind? Do you?"

"Well now...." With one hand I lifted my cap and scratched the top of my head. "I don't want to get in your business but...."

Acknowledgments

I would like to recognize my friends at the Stone Ridge Writing Group for their notes and encouragement, with special appreciation to Catherine Arra for her invaluable input and gentle guidance.

Thank You.

I owe you each a dozen eggs.

Cover illustration by Scott Woods

Contact: Scottleewoods@gmail.com

TheArtofScottWoods.com

Made in the USA
Lexington, KY
08 August 2016